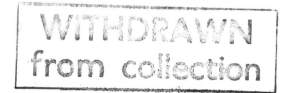
Capturing client requirements in construction projects

John M. Kamara
Chimay J. Anumba
Nosa F. O. Evbuomwan

D1331367

T Thomas Telford

Published by Thomas Telford Publishing, Thomas Telford Ltd, 1 Heron Quay, London, E14 4JD.

URL: http://www.thomastelford.com

Distributors for Thomas Telford books are
USA: ASCE Press, 1801 Alexander Bell Drive, Reston, VA 20191-4400, USA
Japan: Maruzen Co. Ltd, Book Department, 3-10 Nihonbashi 2-chome, Chuo-ku, Tokyo 103
Australia: DA Books and Journals, 648 Whitehorse Road, Mitcham 3132, Victoria

First published 2002

A catalogue record for this book is available from the British Library

ISBN: 0 7277 3103 3

© J. Kamara, C. Anumba, N. Evbuomwan and Thomas Telford Limited, 2002

Typeset by Alex Lazarou, Surbiton, Surrey
Printed and bound in Great Britain by MPG Books, Bodmin, Cornwall

Foreword

The construction industry is a vital part of the UK economy. It accounts for about 10% of the gross domestic product (GDP), over 40% of gross domestic fixed capital formation (GDFCF) in dwellings and other new buildings and works, and employs around 7–12% of the total work force. At the heart of the industry are its clients, who initiate and finance construction projects.

The acknowledged importance of clients as the driving force in the construction industry has led to repeated calls for the construction industry to deliver better value-for-money to its clients. These calls are in response to the criticisms of the industry by clients, who complain that they do not always get what they ask for. While there are many factors, such as project organisation, design, construction and quality of materials, which contribute to client satisfaction, the early stages of construction projects are critical for overall project success.

In addition to these calls for the industry to be more client-focused, clients are also being challenged to be responsible in their dealings with the industry. The 'Client's Charter', which was drawn up by the government-initiated Confederation of Construction Clients (CCC), encourages clients to provide leadership in setting clearly defined and, where possible, quantified objectives and realistic targets for achieving these by the industry. Central to these initiatives is the need for a clear understanding (by both clients and the industry), of the goals and expectations of clients with regard to the facility being commissioned and the minimum standards expected of the industry.

In this regard, it is important that designers and contractors should spend time to understand their clients' business. This is critical as clients expect the industry to provide what they (the clients) want and not what the industry wants to provide. Clients, on their part, must be prepared to work with the supply chain by providing hands-on management, and not just by making demands.

This book describes a methodology for capturing client requirements on construction projects, which facilitates the systematic definition, analysis, and mapping of client requirements to technical design specifications. It addresses a key area (establishment and communication of clients' needs) which was identified by the Construction Research and Innovation Strategy Panel (CRISP) as requiring considerable improvement.

The adoption of the methodology described in the book will allow clients to clearly define and communicate their requirements and expectations for a facility, and link these to their overall business objectives. This will also allow the construction industry to deliver products and services that match and satisfy their clients, thereby providing better value for money.

The principles on which this book is based are very much in line with the Egan agenda of *Rethinking Construction*. I therefore commend this book to all stakeholders in the construction industry — clients, industry practitioners and researchers.

Norman Haste, OBE, FREng
BAA Project Director
Heathrow Terminal 5

Preface

The construction industry has been criticised by both the Latham and Egan reports for often failing to deliver facilities that meet clients' requirements. The problem can be attributed to inadequacies in the conventional briefing process, including, among others, the lack of a systematic and structured methodology, inadequate focus on the client, poor usage of information technology (IT), the use of design solutions to clarify the client's needs, inadequate mechanisms for capturing design intent and rationale, and poor traceability of the client's requirements throughout the project lifecycle.

This book describes an innovative and structured approach for capturing client requirements in construction projects that was developed to overcome the above limitations. The new approach, which is encapsulated in a client requirements processing model (CRPM) (and associated prototype software, ClientPro), facilitates the systematic definition, analysis, and mapping of client requirements to design specifications. It allows for the clarification of a client's business need for a facility, documentation of the rationale for their preferences, and the capture and prioritisation of the perspectives of the interest groups who influence, or are affected by, the proposed facility. It also provides a structured process for prioritising the client's requirements, defining the design solution space (target values), and for translating the 'voice of the client' into measurable design specifications.

The CRPM (and ClientPro) facilitates better understanding and implementation of clients' requirements, more effective collaborative working, and design creativity. It also minimises uncertainties and downstreams problems because of the early consideration of issues affecting the lifecycle of a facility, and it provides the basis for effective requirements management throughout the facility lifecycle.

This book is intended for all parties involved in the construction project delivery process, but will be of particular interest to client's representatives, project managers, development managers, speculative developers, and design managers. It would also be suitable for use as a text for university courses on design briefing and architectural management, as well as other industry sectors interested in customer satisfaction and the use of a structured approach to integrating customer requirements with product design.

Dr John Kamara
Professor Chimay Anumba
Dr Nosa Evbuomwan

Authors' details

Dr John Kamara is a lecturer in the School of Architecture, Planning and Landscape (SAPL), University of Newcastle upon Tyne. Previously he was a research associate at Loughborough University. He graduated in civil engineering in 1985 and, subsequently, pursued postgraduate studies at the University of Newcastle upon Tyne and the University of Teesside. Dr Kamara is a member of the Architectural Informatics group (SAPL), which was established to investigate and understand the role of emergent information technologies in architecture, engineering and construction. He also teaches on the MSc course in digital architecture, which focuses on the increasingly sophisticated use that architects and related professionals must make of computer and communication technologies to work collaboratively and individually in both real and virtual environments. His research interests, which have resulted in over 50 publications, are in the fields of client requirements processing, project development, e-construction, virtual collaborative practice, and knowledge management. Dr Kamara holds membership of the Chartered Institute of Building.

Professor Chimay Anumba is a chartered civil/structural engineer. He is currently Professor of Construction Engineering and Informatics and the founding director of the Centre for Innovative Construction Engineering (CICE) at Loughborough University. His research interests are in the fields of computer-aided engineering, concurrent engineering, IT, knowledge-based systems, collaborative communications, and project management. He has over 150 scientific publications in these fields. Professor Anumba's research work has received widespread support, with a total value of over £10 million from industry, the Engineering and Physical Sciences Research Council (EPSRC), and several UK and international funding bodies. He is actively involved in several professional bodies, and is a member of the governing council of the Institution of Civil Engineers (ICE). Professor Anumba also undertakes advisory and consultancy work for the UK government and construction-sector firms and has recently spent time at both the Massachusetts Institute of Technology (MIT) and Stanford University (Center for Integrated Facility Engineering (CIFE)), USA, as a visiting professor and scholar.

Dr Nosa Evbuomwan is a senior consultant within the SAP practice of Divine Inc., a premier integrated solution provider focused on the extended enterprise, and which provides professional, software and managed services for Global 5000 and high-growth middle market firms, government agencies, and educational institutions. He was a lecturer in structural engineering at the University of Newcastle upon Tyne, research fellow at the Engineering Design Centre at City University, London, and research associate at the University of Birmingham. He also worked as a structural engineer for W. S. Atkins Oil and Gas Engineering Limited, Epsom, and as a lecturer in civil engineering at Bendel (now Edo) State University, Ekpoma, Nigeria. He graduated with a BEng degree in civil engineering from the University of Benin, Benin City, Nigeria, in 1983. Dr Evbuomwan obtained his MSc and DIC degrees in concrete structures from Imperial College, University of London in 1988, and his PhD in engineering and computer-aided design from City University, London, in 1994. His research interests include integrated design and construction, concrete/FRP composite structures, concurrent engineering, design function deployment, business process modelling and integration and computer-aided design. He has published over 80 scientific publications in these fields. He is interested in the use of IT as a competitive tool in industry and has expertise in the construction, manufacturing and healthcare sectors.

Acknowledgements

We are grateful to all those individuals and organisations who contributed to the development of the client requirements processing model (CRPM) and the associated prototype software, ClientPro. We are also indebted to our families, who have been very understanding during the period that it took to put this book together.

Contents

List of figures

List of tables

Chapter 1

Introduction

1.1 Overview of Chapter 1

This chapter sets out the context for capturing clients' requirements in construction. The importance, and need, for client requirements processing are discussed and the requirements for establishing the 'voice of the client' in construction projects are outlined. The chapter concludes with an outline of the objectives of the book and a brief guide to its contents.

1.2 Clients and the construction process

A client can be defined as the person or organisation responsible for commissioning and paying for the design and construction of a facility (e.g. a building, road or bridge), and is usually (but not always) the owner of the facility being commissioned. The client can also be the user of a proposed facility, or they (i.e. the client and user) may be separate entities. However, as the purchaser of services for the design and construction of a facility, the client represents (and should consider) other interests. These include the owner, if different, users and other identified persons, groups or organisations who influence, and are affected by, the acquisition, use, operation and demolition of the proposed facility (e.g. financial institutions, environmental pressure groups and neighbourhood associations). Thus, the 'client' (i.e. buyer of construction services) is a 'body' or 'entity' that incorporates other interests groups (Figure 1.1). The extent to which these are involved depends on the kind and scale of the project. A road project and/or a nuclear power station, for example, will

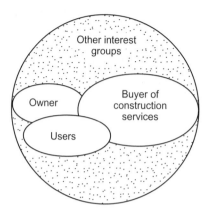

Figure 1.1. Components of the 'client body'

attract the attention of environmental groups; the citing of an entertainment facility, such as a nightclub, in a residential area will have to consider the views of the residents of that neighbourhood.

1.2.1 *Importance of clients to the construction process*

As the initiators and financiers of projects, clients are central to the construction process, and are considered to be the driving force in the construction industry (hereinafter referred to as 'the industry'). Therefore, the ultimate goal of all parties in a project is to satisfy fully the requirements of the client. This invariably depends on the project organisation, design quality, skills of the construction workforce, and the quality and suitability of construction materials (Sanvido *et al.*, 1992). However, the process of satisfying client requirements begins with a clear definition of what those requirements are. This requires a renewed focus on the requirements of the client, and the effective encapsulation of their 'voice' in the design and construction process. An active client's role (e.g. appropriate involvement in project implementation, adequate and timely provision of funds, etc.) is also required, as this is considered to be crucial for project success (Kometa *et al.*, 1995).

1.2.2 *The 'voice of the client'*

The 'voice of the client' is similar to the concept of the 'voice of the customer' which is used in the manufacturing sector to describe the active and systematic process of establishing and incorporating the 'true' wishes of customers in the development of products (Griffin and Hauser, 1991). The 'voice of the client' (or client requirements) includes the collective wishes, perspectives and expectations of the various components of the client body. These requirements describe the facility that will satisfy the client's objectives (or business need). Client requirements constitute the primary source of information for a construction project and, therefore, are of vital importance to the successful planning and implementation of a project.

The need for establishing and adequately incorporating the 'voice of the client' reflects the changes within the construction industry. This need has led to repeated calls for the construction process to be more client-oriented (Latham, 1994; Howie, 1996; Egan, 1998). Construction professionals usually designed with the needs of the environment, aesthetics and posterity in mind, not so much that of the client (Latham, 1994); the effect being that the resulting facilities fall short of the expectations of clients. However, with the increasing sophistication of clients and the general recognition of their pivotal role in the construction process, the industry is now required to deliver better value for money by renewing its focus on client requirements, among other measures (Egan, 1998). Although various client groups (e.g. the British Property Federation (BPF)) have developed initiatives on how they want to procure their projects (BPF, 1983), the onus on developing innovative ways to establish and encapsulate the 'voice of the client' in construction projects, rests with the industry. This is because ultimate blame for defective work and/or poor functioning of facilities is usually put on the industry (Architects' Journal, 1980). Furthermore, as a service provider, the industry should seek to be client-focused. A first step in this direction is the effective 'processing' of client requirements.

1.3   Client requirements processing

The expression of the needs of a client in a form that describes the facility that he or she desires involves some form of 'processing'. Where the client is likely to express his or her needs in non-design terms (as in construction), it then becomes necessary to 'translate' them into design terms. Therefore, client requirements processing involves the *presentation of information* in a format that enhances the *understanding* of precisely what the client desires. It can be formally defined as the definition, analysis, and translation of explicit and implicit client requirements into solution-neutral design specifications. Client requirements need to be processed because of the complexity of clients, their expectations, the nature of project requirements, and the need for collaborative working among construction professionals.

1.3.1   *The complexity of clients*

The complexity of clients arises from the nature of their organisations and their experience with the industry (i.e. the frequency with which they commission projects). Client organisations vary with respect to size, composition and the nature of their business. They can range from a simple family unit commissioning an extension to their dwelling to big multinational corporations or local and central governments. For all these categories, there is a 'business need' (e.g. the need for more space, better communication, etc.) that influences the decision to commission a project. In many cases, and particularly for corporate clients, this decision is not based on an individual's decision but on organisational factors (Kometa and Olomolaiye, 1997). The influence of 'organisational' factors creates complexity because organisations represent different perspectives (e.g. those of different departments or business units) which can be quite conflicting (Cherns and Bryant, 1984). The business need underpinning the decision to commission a project can also conflict with the wishes and perspectives of other components within the client body (Figure 1.1). For example, a corporate decision to rationalise space through open-plan offices might conflict with the users' need for privacy. When the different perspectives within each component of the client body (e.g. different categories of users, etc.) are also taken into consideration, the result is multi-layers of complexity. This is exacerbated further if these components are different organisational entities. Even in the case of 'simple clients' (i.e. those who have no other interest but their own), there is a degree of complexity because of potentially different perspectives, say, between members of a household wishing to extend their house (Walker, 1989).

Complexity can also arise from the 'experience' of the client concerned. Various studies show that the relative ease with which clients' requirements are processed is related to the experience of the client with the industry (Newman *et al.*, 1981; Latham, 1994; DoE, 1995a). When combined with the nature of the client organisation, the relative degree of complexity can be illustrated in Figure 1.2. A very inexperienced client with a complex organisation will pose a more difficult situation for establishing the 'voice of the client' than a more experienced client with a

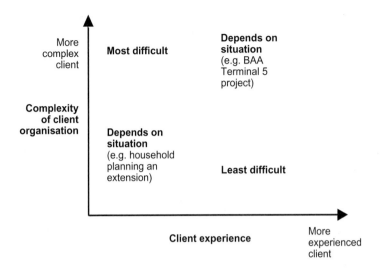

Figure 1.2. Effect of client experience and organisation on requirements processing

relatively less complex organisation. It should be noted, however, that each situation is unique and other factors, such as the skill and experience of industry professionals, and the nature and complexity of the project under consideration, also need to be considered. The implication for establishing and encapsulating the 'voice of the client' therefore involves identifying and resolving the different perspectives within the client body.

1.3.2 Nature of client expectations

Processing of client requirements is also required because of the need to determine their expectations for a project and the resulting facility. Clients are most likely to be satisfied when their perception of the services provided in a facility, which is usually different from that of construction professionals, matches or exceeds their expectations (Ahmed and Kangari, 1995). Although client requirements are unique in every given situation, they can be classified as: basic or expected needs, articulated or demanded needs, and exciting needs (Griffin and Houser, 1991; Mallon and Mulligan, 1993). Basic needs are those that are not voiced but are assumed to be present in a facility (e.g. the expectation that a building will be structurally sound). The fulfilment of basic needs would not excite the client but their omission will reduce his or her satisfaction. Articulated needs are those that are voiced or demanded (e.g. a special feature in a building). Exciting needs are those which, although not voiced, will pleasantly surprise and delight the client if fulfilled (e.g. completing a project under budget). To fully satisfy clients, all three categories of needs must be fulfilled. Therefore, effective processing is required to understand fully the expectations of clients.

1.3.3   Client and project requirements

Another reason why it is necessary to 'process' client requirements is that, within the context of the project in which they are implemented, there are also other requirements, which include:

- site requirements
- environmental requirements
- regulatory requirements
- design and construction requirements.

A brief description of these types of requirements is presented in Table 1.1.

The interrelationship between project requirements is illustrated in Figure 1.3. Client requirements combine with site, environmental and regulatory requirements to produce design requirements, which, in turn, generate construction requirements. Other project requirements are generated (or derive) from the business need of the client that is to be satisfied by the proposed facility. For example, a client's desire to have an office block in a strategic location (because of the nature of his or her business activities) will have an effect on the site, environmental and regulatory (relevant planning regulations) requirements. This suggests that other project requirements can either pose constraints to client requirements or they can enhance their satisfaction. Therefore, an adequate understanding of client requirements (through effective processing) can facilitate the level of trade-offs required with other project requirements, which are usually more difficult to alter than client requirements.

1.3.4   The need for integration and collaborative working

The need for client requirements processing also arises from the need for integrated business strategies within the construction process, and the need for collaborative working among project participants. Integration and collaboration are seen as necessary to improve the efficiency of the

Table 1.1. The different requirements represented in a project

Type of requirements	Meaning
Client requirements	Requirements of the client which describe the facility that satisfies his or her business need. Incorporates user requirements, those of other interest groups and the lifecycle requirements for operating, maintaining and disposing of the facility
Site requirements	These describe the characteristics of the site on which the facility is to be built (e.g. ground conditions, existing services, history, etc.)
Environmental requirements	These describe the immediate environment (climatic factors, neighbourhood, environmental conservation, etc.) surrounding the proposed site for the facility
Regulatory requirements	Building, planning, health and safety regulations, and other legal requirements that influence the acquisition, existence, operation and demolition of the facility
Design requirements	Requirements for design, which are a translation of the client needs, site and environmental requirements
Construction requirements	Requirements for actual construction, which derive from the design activity

construction industry, which is otherwise plagued with the problems associated with the fragmentation of the construction process (Howard *et al.*, 1989; Ashworth, 1991; Brandon and Betts, 1995; Evbuomwan and Anumba, 1996a). Fragmentation in the industry is exacerbated by the sequential 'over the wall' syndrome (Figure 1.4), whereby professionals who are involved in 'downstream' activities (e.g. contractors) are usually not involved in 'upstream' decisions (design) that are passed on to them over the 'wall' of separation between those disciplines. Client requirements, for example, are elicited by design professionals (usually architects) who interpret them and pass on their decisions to the next professional down the chain (e.g. structural engineers). However, the use of integrated strategies, such as design and build and concurrent engineering (a concept from manufacturing that is seen as key to the

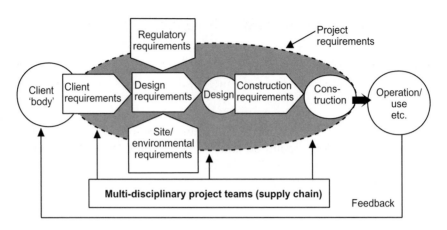

Figure 1.3. Interrelationships between project requirements

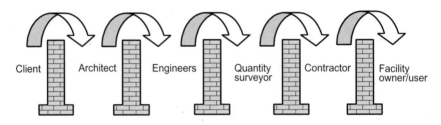

Figure 1.4. Sequential 'over the wall' syndrome for building projects

integration of the construction process — Evbuomwan and Anumba,
1996b; Kamara *et al.*, 2000) requires that client requirements have to be
processed and presented in a manner that will facilitate
concurrent/collaborative working. In the context of multidisciplinary teams,
where the focus, perspective and orientation of each discipline is usually
different, this implies that the presentation of requirements has to be neutral
enough to allow different professionals to understand them in the same way
(not an interpreted version from the perspective of another professional, as in
the sequential 'over the wall' system). This can be done if the requirements are
processed adequately from the format in which the client presents them to a
format that enables a multidisciplinary team to work collaboratively.

1.4 Requirements for establishing the 'voice of the client'

The goals for establishing the 'voice of the client' derive from the need for client requirements processing, which was discussed in the previous sections. These include the following:

1. To address the complexities within the client body through the identification, resolution and incorporation of the different perspectives within the client body.
2. To clarify the objectives and expectations of the client to ensure that they are understood from the perspectives of the client.
3. To focus exclusively on client requirements so as to understand how other project requirements can either enhance or constrain their implementation.
4. To translate and present client requirements in a format that will allow collaborative working and the development, verification and management of appropriate design and construction solutions, which satisfy the objectives of the client.

To satisfy these goals, an appropriate framework for establishing client requirements is required. This framework should ensure that the *process* and the *outputs* of the system satisfy the goals for client requirements processing. The requirements for such a system are outlined below.

1.4.1 Requirements for the 'framework' of a requirements processing system

The framework for client requirements processing can be part of an integrated project environment, or it can serve as an input into the design and construction process (Sanvido *et al.*, 1990; Sanvido and Norton, 1994; Evbuomwan and Anumba, 1995). As part of an integrated project environment, client requirements processing should reflect the manner of working within that environment. The *process* should also ensure that the *outputs* are in line with the goals for establishing the 'voice of the client', outlined above. In particular, it should facilitate:

*   the processing of client requirements for different client and project types

- the identification, incorporation and prioritisation of the different perspectives within the client body through the use of appropriate elicitation and decision-making tools
- the participation and integration of a multidisciplinary team in defining the requirements of the client to eliminate, or minimise, any tendencies towards the 'over the wall' syndrome
- the capture, verification and management of all relevant information (e.g. issues relating to the lifecycle of the facility) pertaining to the objectives, needs and expectations of the client.
- the integration of client requirements processing with other activities in the construction process.

It is also essential that a framework for client requirements processing is computer-based, in order to realise the full benefits of computer-integrated construction (Howard *et. al.*, 1989; Miyatake and Kangari, 1993; Evbuomwan and Anumba, 1996a). A computer-based client requirements processing framework is vital for integration with information technology (IT) based downstream activities in construction. The use and implementation of structured methodologies are also better managed using IT tools. Furthermore, conformance checking and traceability of requirements throughout the project lifecycle can be done automatically if requirements processing is computer based.

1.4.2 Requirements for the output of a requirements processing system

As an input to design, client requirements processing provides an interface between a client's demands and the measures (design and construction) used by the industry to meet those demands (Worthington, 1994; Gibson *et al.*, 1995). Therefore, the *nature* and *content* of the information that constitutes the 'voice of the client' (i.e. how it is expressed or stated) should facilitate the development of appropriate solutions (design and otherwise) to the client's problem, and should enhance the work of an integrated project team. Therefore, client requirements should be:

- clear and unambiguous, to minimise or eliminate any confusion arising from multiple interpretations of their meaning — clarity can also facilitate the verification and management of client requirements throughout the lifecycle of the project/facility (Perkinson *et al.*, 1994)

- comprehensive — that is, they should incorporate, as much as possible, the collective wishes and expectations of the different components of the client and issues relating to the lifecycle of the facility (e.g. its acquisition, operation, use, management, disposal, etc.) should also be included
- solution-neutral, to allow innovation and creativity in devising solutions to the client's problem
- stated in a format that can be understood by the different disciplines working on a project — this goes beyond understanding requirements from the perspective of the client and it involves the presentation (or translation) of client requirements to satisfy the information needs of the different disciplines represented in an integrated project team. This also requires that requirements are processed and categorised to the same level of granularity for adequate and effective prioritisation by removing as much fuzziness as possible.

1.5. The objective and contents of the book

This book presents an innovative and structured approach to the processing of clients requirements that satisfies the requirements for establishing the 'voice of the client' described above. This approach was developed in response to the need for an appropriate mechanism for client requirements processing. The need is partly due to the inadequacies of the existing process of briefing, which does not provide an appropriate framework for the effective processing of client requirements. It is also partly due to the limitations of the improvements to the briefing process that are being proposed, which do not go far enough to solve the problem (Kamara and Anumba, 2001). The development, application and evaluation of this methodology are described in subsequent chapters, as follows:

- Chapter 2 reviews the existing process for briefing in construction and assesses its effectiveness in establishing the 'voice of the client' in construction projects with respect to the requirements outlined in this chapter
- Chapter 3 explores the different tools and methodologies that can be used to establish the 'voice of the client' in construction projects — it reviews various techniques with particular focus on quality

function deployment (QFD), and describes how these can be integrated for client requirements processing

- Chapter 4 presents the methodology for client requirements processing — it describes how it was developed and provides details of the various stages required for processing client requirements
- Chapter 5 discusses the application of the client requirements processing model (CRPM) within the context of the construction process — examples of how the CRPM can be used in practice are also presented
- Chapter 6 describes the development of a software application (ClientPro) that implements the CRPM within a computer environment — the use and evaluation of the system by construction industry practitioners are also discussed
- Chapter 7 summarises and draws conclusions from the book — it also discusses the benefits of the CRPM and its associated software prototype, ClientPro, and outlines the future work required to enhance its usability.

Chapter 2

Briefing and client requirements processing

2.1 Overview of Chapter 2

This chapter appraises the current process of briefing in the UK construction industry and assesses its effectiveness in establishing the 'voice of the client' in construction projects. It reviews the literature on briefing, and presents and discusses the findings from studies on briefing. These findings are used to assess the effectiveness of the briefing processing in establishing the 'voice of the client'.

2.2 The briefing process

The briefing process in construction is the process through which a client informs others of his or her needs, aspirations and desires for a project (CIB, 1997). The document that contains the written instructions/requirements of the client is referred to as the 'brief' which, according to various authors (e.g. Salisbury, 1990; Worthington, 1994; CIT, 1996; CIB 1997), should include information (in varying levels of detail) on:

- the background, purpose, scope, content and desired outcomes of the project
- the functions of the intended facility and the relationships between them
- cost and time targets, instructions on procurement and organisation of the project

- site and environmental conditions, safety, interested third parties, and other factors that are likely to influence the design and construction of a facility.

The development of briefs (i.e. briefing) is influenced by various factors that are related to the information required, the nature of the project, type and size of client, and the skills of those involved in the process (Newman *et al.*, 1981; Worthington, 1994). Complex projects require much more information, involve many multidisciplinary professionals and, therefore, may present greater challenges for briefing. Similarly, inexperienced client organisations may also find it relatively difficult to define their requirements in briefing (Kamara *et al.*, 1996). However, irrespective of the nature of the project and client organisation, the briefing stage constitutes an initial phase (or activity) of the construction process and provides the link between clients and the industry (RIBA, 1973; BPF, 1983; ICE, 1996a). It also contributes towards project success and ultimate client satisfaction (Sanvido *et al.*, 1992; Worthington, 1994). Although a good brief is not an end in itself, it would be very difficult, if not impossible, to design and construct a facility that fully satisfies a client without a good brief that clearly and unambiguously states those requirements (Sharpe, 1972; Latham, 1994, MacLeod *et al.*, 1998).

The importance of effective briefing is reflected in the many briefing guides (e.g. RIBA, 1973; Palmer, 1981; BPF, 1983; Parsloe, 1990; Salisbury, 1990; ICE, 1996a; CIB, 1997) that have been developed to aid practitioners in the formulation of briefs. It is also reflected in the number of studies (e.g. Newman *et al.*, 1981; Goodacre *et. al.*, 1982; Kelly *et al.*, 1992; Barret, 1996; CIT, 1996; Kumar, 1996; Yusuf, 1997, Morris *et al.*, 1998) that have been conducted to either understand the process, and/or develop new ways to improve it. These studies also reveal that although the briefing process is important, it does have limitations in providing an adequate framework for establishing the requirements of clients.

2.3   Studies on briefing

The methodology adopted in appraising the briefing process involved a mixture of both qualitative and quantitative research methods (Bryman, 1989; Miller, 1991). Specifically, this included a review of literature, informal interviews and discussions with construction industry professionals and other academics involved in briefing research, detailed case studies of the briefing process, and a questionnaire survey of a random sample of clients and consultants in the industry.

2.3.1 Case studies

Case studies of the briefing processes adopted by four organisations were conducted using semi-structured interviews. These provided insight into how the briefing process is organised in specific organisations and projects (depth). The following approach was generally adopted:

- initial contact with interviewees
- in-depth interviews, which were recorded on tape
- review of relevant documents supplied by interviewees
- further discussions (usually over the phone) to clarify any difficulties
- writing of report, comments, feedback, amendments and confirmation of report.

2.3.2 Industry survey

In addition to the case studies, the views of 63 client organisations and 84 consulting firms were surveyed (by postal questionnaires) to obtain information about the briefing process (Som, 1973; Hague, 1993; Rudduck, 1995). Client organisations were selected at random from a list drawn from several issues of the *Contracts Journal* (1995). Consulting firms were also selected at random from the Royal Institute of British Architects' (RIBA) list of practices (RIBA, 1995) and the Institution of Civil Engineers' (ICE) *Consultants File* (NCE, 1996). The focus of the survey was to solicit information on the briefing practice adopted for specific projects in which the respondents played a part. Respondents were asked to tick either 'yes', 'no' or 'not sure' to a list of statements for up to five projects that they had been involved in recently. There was also provision for comments on each statement, and on how to improve the briefing process. Various literature sources, discussions with industry professionals, and a pilot survey provided the basis for the statements presented in the survey. The questionnaires to clients and consultants were basically the same, except for the details about their organisations.

2.4   Description of results

2.4.1   Case studies

The details of the organisations involved in the case studies are listed in Table 2.1, which shows the type of business, number of employees, annual turnover in pounds sterling, project/property portfolio, and the basis of the case study in each organisation. Table 2.2 presents a summary of the findings about briefing from these organisations and outlines the general procedure adopted (including those involved in the process), the collection of information and some notable observations about the briefing process in each organisation. It should be noted that these studies were not intended to be representative of briefing practices generally, but rather served to provide depth of insight into the briefing process of particular organisations or within a particular project (as in organisation C in Tables 2.1 and 2.2).

2.4.2   Industry survey

The overall response to the postal survey was 17% (17·5% for clients and 16·7% for consultants) out of a total of 147 questionnaires. Of the clients who responded, 46% were developers, 27% were commercial firms who had commissioned projects, 18% were educational institutions and 9% were government institutions (Figure 2.1). Among the consultants, 29% were architectural firms in the private and public sector, 21% were civil/structural engineering firms (private and public sectors), 42% were multidisciplinary practices (architects, civil/structural and services engineers, project managers, and quantity surveyors), while 7% were project management firms.

2.4.2.1   Type of projects represented in the survey

A total of 117 projects were reported on and 74·4% of these were building projects, 19·7% were civil engineering projects and 5·9% were other projects that could not be categorised as building or civil engineering (e.g. children's play area) — see Figure 2.2. A majority of these projects were procured using traditional contracts, which are characterised by the separation of design and construction (53%), 34·2% were procured by design and build, 7·7% by management contracting, and 5·1% by other procurement methods (e.g. construction management). The value of most

Table 2.1. Details of organisations involved in case studies

Organisation	Type of business	Number of employees	Annual turnover: £ million	Project/property portfolio	Basis of case study
A	Airport company	8000	1200	£500 million annually on new/improved facilities	Organisational briefing process
B	Charity	5000	100	Manages over 850 properties (including 300 high street shops)	Organisational briefing process
C	University	1600	51	88 000 m^2 of floor space; £2·5 million to £15 million* annually on its estate	Specific project (building project)
D	Architectural practice	180	5	Involved in about 400 projects annually	Organisational briefing process

* Normal expenditure is around £2·5 million; the cost of new projects (funded externally) in recent years amounted to about £15 million

Table 2.2. Summary of briefing process in various organisations

	Organisation A	Organisation B	Organisation C (building project)	Organisation D
General procedure	Structured approach to briefing for projects over a certain limit that is part of a project process Three types of briefs used: strategic brief (for feasibility studies), outline brief (for concept design) and detailed brief (brief for coordinated design) Each brief is divided into two parts: a statement of requirements (SOR) — documents strategic requirements; and a basis of design (BOD) — translates SOR into technical specifications Preparation of each brief follows review and sign-off process of the preceding stage in project process	Formal briefing process for projects over a certain limit Process involves two main stages: part 1 and part 2 briefs Part 1 brief is a statement of needs and forms basis for feasibility studies, acquisition of site — high-level managers, architects and portfolio managers are involved at this stage Part 2 brief is used for the design and development of a facility (e.g. general design considerations, etc.) and a broader mix of professionals are involved including, in some cases, end users of the proposed facility	Project (refurbishment of existing building) initiated by an academic school within the university, but other groups became involved Brief developed through a series of meetings between client representatives and members of the design team; meetings with some user-groups (not including students) were also held Faxes, internal memos and visits to similar facilities were also used to communicate/approve client requirements Other meetings (e.g. of design and project teams) to discuss/approve briefing reports	Primarily involved in architectural design but also offers exclusive briefing services that do not include design (35–40% of its commissions) No specific format for briefing — style and approach adopted depends on type of client, project and scope of work However, a briefing and design plan is used as checklist for the kind of actions to be taken and information to be collected in any particular job Specialist brief writers are primarily involved in brief formulation

Information collected	Similar structure of information for both parts of each brief Level of information becomes more detailed as process continues	General information on project and end-users are presented during part 1; more detailed information with respect to design is presented in part 2 brief	Sketchy information (outline brief) on the general requirements of project initiator; supplementary brief to include the concerns of other groups	Briefing information collected through workshops, interviews, questionnaires; particular focus is placed on understanding the nature of the client organisation
Notable points	Standard format and well-defined procedure for briefing Communication of client requirements through an iterative process of briefing, designing, reviewing and 'fixing' Use of structured methods in decision making, and deliberate attempt to 'translate' strategic needs into technical specifications	Significant role of architects in brief formulation — other professionals only provide input Use of questionnaires to collect briefing information, and the use of design to clarify requirements Minimal involvement (input) from end-users in brief formulation Combining briefing with design is not necessarily helpful in understanding client requirements	Need for project funding introduced other stakeholders — this created complexities and conflicts in the briefing process Organisation of briefing around meetings and consultations Dominance of one of the client groups (i.e. the school that initiated the project) Collection of some briefing information in arrears	Tendency for programme to drive a project rather than client requirements Briefing decisions are sometimes not recorded Need for some flexibility of client requirements — very detailed and prescriptive brief is usually not helpful Combining briefing with design is not always adequately representing client interests

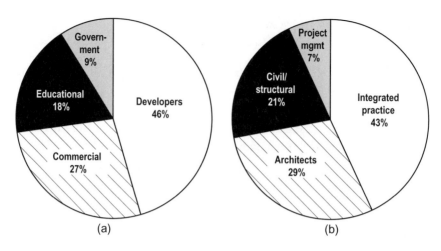

Figure 2.1. Proportion of respondents to questionnaire survey: (a) clients; and (b) consultants

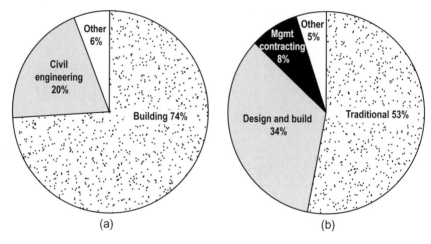

Figure 2.2. Description of projects represented in the survey: (a) project type; and (b) contract type

of the projects was under £10 million; most were of less than five years in duration.

2.4.2.2 Responses to specific statements

Table 2.3 presents the responses to the statements presented in the survey. From these responses it is seen that no formal briefing

Table 2.3. Responses to statements about briefing

Statement	Responses (per cent of 117 projects)		
	Yes	No	Not sure
The briefing evolved with the design	48·3	44·9	6·8
Briefing was started after the decision to 'build'	47·3	46·4	6·3
No formal procedures were used in the briefing process	29·6	58·2	12·2
The initial brief described the basic objectives of the client (statement of needs)	71·8	28·2	
The functional brief described the client's specific requirements	44·9	44·9	10·2
Briefing involved the translation of client needs into detailed design specifications	61·6	25	13·4
No formal procedure was used to translate needs into specifications	28·9	50	21·1
Sketches and drawings were used to translate needs into specifications	53·6	37·3	9·1
Computer tools were used in translating needs into specifications	52·1	43·8	4·1
The RIBA plan of work was used as the guide for preparing the brief	32·5	67·5	
The ICE project guidelines were used in developing the brief	13·6	78·8	7·6
The requirements were precisely defined before design started	56·3	39·7	4
A structured methodology was used to analyse and prioritise requirements	28·1	62	9·9
A rigorous analysis of client requirements was carried out during briefing	38·5	55	6·5
The feasibility study focused on evaluating possible solutions	47·4	45·6	7·0

Table 2.3. continued

Statement	Responses (per cent of 117 projects)		
	Yes	No	Not sure
The feasibility study focused on assessing site conditions	64·0	29·0	7·0
The feasibility study focused on assessing environmental factors likely to affect the project	51·7	38·1	10·2
The feasibility study focused on legal and regulatory factors likely to affect the project	62·4	35·9	1·7
Site conditions were a constraint on the client's requirements	54·8	41·2	4·0
Environmental factors were a constraint on the client's requirements	39·5	56·5	4·0
Regulatory requirements were a constraint on the client's requirements	59·5	40·5	
Changes to requirements were recorded as corrections to drawings	75·4	23	1·6
Changes to requirements were recorded on a sheet of paper in a file	56	29·3	14·7
It was relatively easy to maintain an audit trail of client requirements during design	52·1	38	9·9
It was relatively easy to maintain an audit trail of client requirements during construction	65·3	28·9	5·8
Combining briefing with design enhanced a thorough understanding of client needs	65	29·9	5·1
Briefing information was layered from general to specific (e.g. spaces to room data)	33	58·3	8·7
Briefing information was elicited sequentially (e.g. room details after spaces, etc.)	26·2	58·9	14·9
Downstream briefing information constrained by predetermined up-stream information	14·4	53·2	32·4

Table 2.3. continued

Statement	Responses (per cent of 117 projects)		
	Yes	No	Not sure
There was effective integration within each briefing stage (horizontal integration)	27·8	36·1	36·1
There was effective integration between briefing stages (vertical integration)	34·5	26·9	38·6
All project consultants were actively involved in defining the client's requirements	46·3	46·3	7·4
You were fully satisfied with the briefing process for the project	34·7	51·2	14·1

procedures were used in 58·2% of the projects surveyed. The translation of a client's needs into detailed design specifications is the key activity in briefing for 61·6% of projects in the survey. In 53·6% of projects, sketches and drawings were used to translate client needs into design specifications and the precise definition of client requirements before detailed design was done in 56·3% of the projects surveyed. A structured methodology, to analyse and prioritise client requirements, was used in only 28·1% of the projects. Changes to requirements were mostly made as corrections to drawings in 75·4% of cases, and respondents indicated that it was relatively easy to maintain an audit trail of client requirements during design (52·1%) and construction (65·3%). In 65% of the projects, respondents maintained that combining briefing with design facilitated a thorough understanding of the client's requirements, although the elicitation of briefing information was undertaken in a haphazard way (i.e. not done in stages) in most cases (58·9% of projects). In up to 38·6% of projects, it was not clear whether there was horizontal integration (i.e. integration within each stage in the briefing process) and vertical integration (i.e. between stages in the briefing process). Overall, respondents were not fully satisfied with the briefing process in over 65% of projects.

2.4.2.3   Comments on how to improve the briefing process

Table 2.4 provides the list of comments made by both clients and respondents on how to improve the briefing process. Suggestions included:

- clarity in defining client requirements
- more involvement of various actors (e.g. client, job architect, quantity surveyor, etc.)

Table 2.4. List of comments on how to improve the briefing process

Clients	Consultants
Job architect was appointed after the brief was prepared — before would have been better	More client input
	Improve integration within each stage of the briefing process
	Client needs to be more realistic: match ambitions with budget
	More time to assess the impact of the client's evolving requirements
Clients must have a clear understanding of what they require	The quantity surveyor should be more involved
	A sign-off procedure when passing from one stage to the next
	Virtual reality computer model link required
Consultants should respond accurately to the client's input	Project team meetings commencing at an early stage and throughout the project, and improved project management
	More thought and communication by lead client with users
Clear and concise brief from the client	Less modification of requirements during design and construction
	Improved education of clients in the briefing process
	More realistic time-scales defined at outset of project

- definitive sign-off procedures for decision making
- adequate incorporation of client's views in design.

The comments suggest that there are limitations in the briefing process; these are discussed later in the book.

2.5   General findings about briefing

The case studies and industry survey described above provide an insight into the briefing process. This mixture of qualitative and quantitative methods ensured that results are fairly indicative of industry practice and, therefore, can be used to make a fair assessment of the general process of briefing in the construction industry.

2.5.1   Briefing procedure

Briefing is a *process*, which constitutes a set of linked activities that take an input (information) and transform it to create an output (brief). Therefore, the framework for discussion will be in terms of the linked activities that convert inputs into outputs, the means by which this conversion is made, the ways in which information is collected, communicated and documented, and the decision-making process involved. It will also be with respect to the contribution of briefing to the satisfaction of client requirements.

2.5.2   Stages in briefing

Briefing is combined with conceptual and scheme design (Figure 2.3). The brief is layered and becomes focused as the design gets progressively fixed. Therefore, the stages in the process can be blurred. However, there are at least two stages: an initial (strategic, part one, etc.) brief which evolves into a detailed (project, part two, etc.) brief. Each subsequent brief is a development of the previous one and becomes more detailed, as the design progresses. The apparent preference for an evolving brief is corroborated by an earlier study on briefing that arrived at a similar conclusion (Goodacre *et al.*, 1982). However, from the survey, and from continued discussions with industry practitioners, there appears to be a growing desire for more definitive briefs; or rather, procedures for the effective sign-off of decisions.

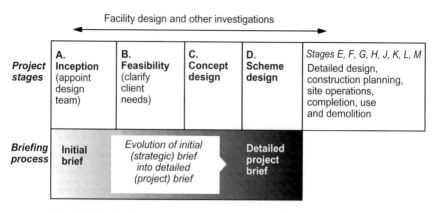

Facility design and other investigations

Project stages	A. Inception (appoint design team)	B. Feasibility (clarify client needs)	C. Concept design	D. Scheme design	Stages E, F, G, H, J, K, L, M Detailed design, construction planning, site operations, completion, use and demolition
Briefing process	Initial brief	Evolution of initial (strategic) brief into detailed (project) brief		Detailed project brief	

Note: Lettering of project stages correspond to the RIBA classification (RIBA, 1973)

Figure 2.3. Briefing within the overall project process

2.5.3 Collection and documentation of information

Information is collected using a variety of methods, which include:

- interviews
- workshops
- electronic equipment for space–time utilisation studies
- continuous discussions
- examination of client documents (e.g. minutes of meetings, memoranda, etc.)
- evaluation of existing facilities
- visits to similar facilities.

The information collected is sometimes recorded in formal documents, which can be in the form of correspondence (letters, faxes, e-mail), minutes of meetings, sketches and drawings, etc. However, unless a very structured process is used, these documents are not normally stored together as part of the 'brief'. In some cases, there is no proper documentation, and the design team relies on recollections of verbal communications with the client. For example, a sole practitioner architect working in the country with an average of about ten commissions a year commented that he had 'not had a written brief for 30 years and sometimes the first time [he] see[s] a client's signature is when the cheque is paid'.

2.5.4   *Processing of information*

A process of 'trial and error', through the use of sketches and drawings, is used mostly to clarify the client's problem, or process briefing information. However, there are situations where clients who commission many projects define their requirements before design (e.g. organisation A in Table 2.1). The survey revealed that in 56·3% of projects, the requirements are defined clearly before design. Although it was not clear which stage in the design process was being referred to, further contacts and discussions indicated that the requirements are defined clearly before detailed design (i.e. after concept and scheme design). The processing of briefing information also involves detailed research, site investigations and building surveys to determine specific information for the project.

2.5.5   *Those involved in briefing*

A broad mix of professionals are involved in briefing. These professionals can either be based in the client organisation or they can represent firms within the construction industry. They include:

- administrators (managers)
- architects
- development managers
- engineers (building services, civil and structural)
- planning supervisors
- portfolio managers
- project managers
- quantity surveyors.

In spite of this range of professionals, there is a tendency for design professionals (e.g. architects and engineers) to play a dominant part in the early stages of briefing. In fact, one of the comments from the survey was that 'quantity surveyors are not adequately involved in the briefing process'.

2.5.6   *Decision making in briefing*

In briefing, decisions have to be made on what constitutes a correct representation of the client's requirements (the problem), and the representation of those requirements in design terms (the solution). This usually involves the resolution of competing interests between different groups within the client body (as in the project by organisation C in Table 2.1), and between professionals with diverse perspectives. Decisions are usually the result of discussions and negotiations between those involved in the briefing process. In some cases, techniques such as value management (e.g. Organisation A in Table 2.1) are used to assist the decision-making process. However, in a majority of cases (62% in the survey) the resolution of conflicts within requirements is done subjectively, without the use of a structured methodology to analyse and prioritise client requirements.

2.5.7   Management of the briefing process

The management of changes and the traceability of requirements are influenced by the way requirements are represented in subsequent stages of the briefing and design process. Changes to requirements are managed by recording them as corrections to sketches and drawings, the main medium for representing the brief (75·4% of projects represented in the survey). These changes may also be discussed in meetings (e.g. project team meetings and evaluation workshops) and decisions recorded in the reports of those meetings. The format of the stage C and D reports (RIBA, 1973) (see Figure 2.3) also makes provision for a summary of the client's brief, and other information such as the sources of the brief (e.g. minutes of meetings, telephone conversations, etc.), space requirements and the rationale for the design. This is intended to facilitate the traceability of client requirements.

2.5.8   Effectiveness of the current process

The briefing process, as currently practised, does not seem to provide the optimum in defining and understanding the client's needs. Respondents indicated that in a majority of projects (65%), combining briefing with design facilitated a thorough understanding of the client's needs. However, in over 65% of projects, respondents could not describe their assessment of the briefing process as entirely satisfactory. These may be due to a number of limitations in the briefing process, which are discussed in the next section.

2.6   Briefing and client requirements processing

The findings from the research on briefing indicate that there are limitations in current practice and in the framework for briefing.

2.6.1   Limitations in the practice of briefing

The suggestions from some respondents in the survey (Table 2.4) provide an insight into the problems in current briefing practice. The problems identified from the case studies and the industry survey include the following:

- inadequate involvement of all the relevant parties to a project
- insufficient time allocated for briefing
- inadequate consideration of the perspectives of the client
- inadequate communication between those involved in briefing
- inadequate management of changes in requirements.

These problems, which are supported by other studies on briefing (e.g. Newman *et al.*, 1981; Goodacre *et al.*, 1982; Kelly *et al.*, 1992; Barrett, 1996; CIT, 1996), may partly be due to the attitude or inefficiencies of those involved, but they also suggest that the general framework for briefing is inadequate.

2.6.2   Limitations in the framework for briefing

The limitations in the existing framework for briefing, which are discussed below, can shift the focus away from the requirements of the client, and can result in problems in briefing practice.

2.6.2.1   The nature of project requirements

Briefing deals with the collection of information for project implementation and, often, project requirements are taken to be the same as client requirements. However, project requirements consist of many types of requirements (client, user, site, environmental, regulatory, design, construction and lifecycle requirements) (Kamara *et al.*, 2000). Client requirements combine with site, environmental and regulatory requirements to produce design requirements, which, in turn, generate construction requirements. Other project requirements can either pose constraints to client requirements, or they can enhance their satisfaction. Therefore, an adequate understanding of client requirements can be achieved if they are considered distinctly from other project requirements. However, if they are considered together, as in current practice, there is the tendency for other requirements (e.g. those of the site) to overshadow client requirements; a case of 'the tail wagging the dog'.

2.6.2.2   Use of the solution to clarify the problem

Current briefing practice tends to be solution-focused. The solution, in the form of sketches and drawings, is used to define the problem. Although this can be interpreted as a difference in the method used to define the problem, a solution-based approach tends to shift the focus from the requirements of the client to that of the designer(s). Proposed solutions are usually made before a thorough understanding of the client's requirements. Therefore, there is an inherent tendency for the client to be influenced by the preferences of the designer(s). In itself, this may not be disadvantageous to the client, who relies on the expertise of the designer to provide a design solution to his or her problem. It is also recognised that the design problem may not entirely precede the solution (Sharpe, 1972; Lawson, 1997). However, since the solution is based on a partial understanding of the problem, the requirements of clients may take second place to that of designers. MacLeod *et al.* (1998) also suggest that 'if one does not know clearly what one is trying to achieve...then the chances of achieving good outcomes must be diminished'. Furthermore, this practice assumes that a design professional has to lead the briefing process (RIBA, 1973). The experience of organisation D (Table 2.1) in this regard is that designers do not necessarily make good brief writers. Besides, briefing is mainly concerned with information, a fact acknowledged by the American Institute of Architects in their guide to facility programming (Palmer, 1981). The assumption that a designer has to lead the process is also at odds with alternative forms of working, such as design and build, and management contracting (Winter, 1989). In effect, a solution-focused approach does not guarantee continued focus on the client, and many briefs are generated out of design rather than a clear understanding of the client's actual objectives (Howie, 1996).

2.6.2.3   Traceability of requirements

The use of sketches and drawings to restate and record changes to client requirements (as in 75·4% of projects represented in the survey) can make it difficult for requirements to be traced to the original needs of the client. Respondents to the questionnaire survey indicated that in 52·1% and 65·3% of projects, it was relatively easy to maintain an audit trail of the client's requirements during design and construction, respectively. In the example of the building project (organisation C in Tables 2.1 and 2.2), changes to requirements were discussed and recorded in periodic project team meetings. However, records of decisions at such project meetings can be quite vague, and do not provide any explanation of why those decisions were taken. Furthermore, an examination of the reports for stages C and D (RIBA, 1973) (see Figure 2.3), suggests that traceability to the original requirements of the client cannot be guaranteed. Although a stage D report for a building project will contain a section on the 'client's brief', which provides a summary of the sources of the brief and other requirements, it is basically a set of design drawings that constitute a proposed solution to the client's problem. In this regard, the framework for briefing does not seem to provide for the unambiguous representation of the client's requirements with respect to his or her problem or business need that will facilitate traceability to the original intentions of the client.

2.6.2.4   *Reflecting the priorities of the client body*

Within the current framework for briefing, the rationalisation and prioritisation of client requirements are done subjectively as the brief evolves with the design. It can be argued that even when objective methods are used, there is still the need for subjective judgements, which are based on the experience of project participants. However, in the absence of any objective and structured methodology, any or all of the following could happen:

- it may not be possible to include most perspectives, particularly that of users, in the decision-making process (as in the project example of organisation C in Table 2.1)
- it may not be possible to establish the relative importance of requirements, or take account of the relative importance of the various interest groups in a project
- designers will not be able to effectively balance the cost of fulfilling a requirement against its relative importance to the client.

Furthermore, when prioritisation is done during concept and scheme design, there is the tendency for client requirements to be obscured by the constraints that are introduced in the design phase. Therefore, prioritisation will not be focused exclusively on the client requirements but will include design considerations as well. If design is to serve as the conceptual solution to the requirements of clients, then the prioritisation of those requirements should be separate from the design process. It is observed that 'while a formal approach to requirements may have been absent in many successful designs, the potential for such action in helping to achieve good design outcomes cannot be denied' (MacLeod *et al.*, 1998).

2.6.2.5   Briefing and project outcomes

It should be noted that limitations in briefing do not necessarily mean that good or even excellent facilities are not achieved in practice. Barrett (1996) suggested that bad examples do yield good results sometimes. The question, however, is whether the wishes of clients and users are satisfied fully. The limitations in briefing do not guarantee this, as the reported cases of client dissatisfaction indicate (Latham, 1994; DoE, 1995b; Egan, 1998). The building project in the case study (organisation C) won an award for innovation. However, not long after its completion, staff members using the facility made a formal protest complaining about the unsuitability of their office accommodation.

2.6.3   The framework for briefing and problems in current practice

It can be seen from the foregoing discussion that the problems in current briefing practice, outlined in Section 2.5 above, are the symptoms of an otherwise flawed framework. For example, if sketches and drawings are to be used to clarify client's requirements, it stands to reason that a professional who has that expertise (an architect, in the case of building projects) will have to produce sketches before other professionals (e.g. a quantity surveyor) are involved. This reinforces the sequential 'over the wall' syndrome of the traditional procurement process, and it is not surprising that there is inadequate involvement of all the relevant parties in the briefing process.

The practice of combining briefing with design can also explain why there is 'insufficient time allocated for briefing'. This is because the pressure on design teams to meet deadlines can minimise the time spent on actually understanding the requirements of the client. Furthermore, as the example of organisation D shows (Table 2.2), not all architects are good brief writers and, therefore, there is the tendency for them to focus on design rather than on clearly establishing the requirements of the client. Other practices, such as the consideration of all project requirements, instead of the exclusive focus of client needs initially, can result in the inadequate consideration of the perspectives of the client, as discussed above.

2.7   Need for effective processing of client requirements

It is to be noted that because of the problems associated with briefing, various initiatives to devise ways to improve it are being attempted. However, these emerging attempts do not offer much as they do not represent any radical changes to the existing framework. For example, the improved process for briefing formulated by the Construction Industry Board (CIB) (CIB, 1997) introduces a pre-project stage that focuses on establishing the client's business needs (strategic brief), but the processing and representation of information is based, as in current practice, on the use of sketches and drawings. Computer-based tools that are being developed (e.g. Kumar, 1996; Yusuf, 1997; Morris *et al.*, 1998) are basically computerised systems of existing practices. Although they might enhance current briefing practices in providing for the completeness of information, they do not provide for the systematic processing of client requirements, nor do they provide for the unambiguous definition and translation of business objects into technical specifications (as is the practice of organisation A — see Table 2.2). Thus, what is required is an effective mechanism, which can ensure that:

- focus on the requirements of the client is maintained throughout the design process
- client requirements are defined clearly and are understood from the perspective of clients (not those of the different professional disciplines)
- client requirements are stated in a format that can make it relatively easy for a design team to act upon them
- there is a mechanism for managing the inevitable changes to requirements, and which allows for tracing and correlating the history of design decisions to the original and evolving requirements of the client.

The discussion of the briefing process in this chapter has considered the 'brief' (as defined previously) as an input to the creative design process and that 'briefing' deals primarily with the processing of information (Sharpe, 1972; Palmer, 1981). Therefore, the focus has been on the 'representation of information' in a manner that maintains focus on client requirements. It is, however, recognised that briefing is usually considered to be part of the creative design process (Worthington, 1994; CIT, 1996; CIB, 1997) and attempts to 'systematise' the way it is carried out cannot always be valid since the design process itself is complex and does not always evolve in a systematic manner (Sharpe, 1972; Lawson, 1997). However, Sharpe (1972) suggests that the arrangement (or processing) of information in a meaningful way can serve as the basis for design synthesis, and can help in the 'incubation' of creative design ideas. Therefore, it is helpful to have a framework that will be useful in:

- helping clients to clarify their vision of the facility to be constructed
- facilitating communication and a common understanding of the client's requirements among members of the requirements processing team and, subsequently, those of the design team
- enhancing collaborative working since there is a common understanding of the client's requirements among members of the design team
- facilitating design creativity since client requirements are translated into a solution-neutral format
- minimising uncertainties that may arise from an unclear definition of client requirements
- minimising downstream problems owing to early consideration of issues affecting the lifecycle of the proposed facility
- providing the basis for effective requirements management throughout the project lifecycle
- ensuring that focus on the client's requirements is maintained.

The development of such a methodology for client requirements processing is the subject of subsequent chapters.

Chapter 3

Tools and methodologies for client requirements processing

3.1 Overview of Chapter 3

It was established in the previous chapter that the current process of briefing does not provide a suitable framework for client requirements processing. Therefore, this chapter explores different methodologies and tools that can be used to establish the 'voice of the client' in construction projects. The approach to requirements definition, analysis and management in other disciplines, such as manufacturing and requirements engineering, provides the basis for identifying appropriate tools for establishing the 'voice of the client' in accordance with the goals defined in Chapter 1. The integration of these tools into a client requirements processing framework is also described.

3.2 Goals for establishing client requirements

The goals for establishing client requirements, which were defined in Chapter 1, are reiterated here for easy reference:

1. To address the complexities within the client body through the identification, resolution and incorporation of the different perspectives within the client body.
2. To clarify the objectives and expectations of the client to ensure that they are understood from the perspectives of the client.
3. To focus exclusively on client requirements so as to understand how other project requirements can either enhance or constrain their implementation.

4. To translate and present client requirements in a format that will allow collaborative working and the development, verification and management of appropriate design and construction solutions, which satisfy the objectives of the client.

The achievement of the above goals requires an appropriate framework for client requirements processing, which will utilise various methodologies and tools. The identification and integration of these tools into a coherent strategy for the establishment of client requirements will begin by a review of requirements processing in the related disciplines of manufacturing and requirements engineering (a subset of software engineering). The practice of looking elsewhere for solutions to the problems in the construction industry is not new, as various initiatives to improve the efficiency of the construction process in the 1990s have focused on modelling construction as a manufacturing process (Sanvido and Medeiros, 1990; Anumba *et al.*, 1995; Crowley, 1996; Egan, 1998). The fact that existing mechanisms for briefing within the industry do not satisfy the goals for establishing client requirements outlined above (see Chapter 2), also suggests that potential solutions from outside the industry need to be investigated.

3.3   Requirements processing in manufacturing

The understanding and fulfilment of customer requirements in the manufacturing industry is closely related to the concept of quality, which is a measure of the extent to which customer requirements and expectations are satisfied (Lochner and Matar, 1990). Thus, insights into the processing of customer requirements in manufacturing can be gained from techniques for incorporating 'quality' into the product development process. These techniques or concepts include:

- total quality management (TQM)
- robust design
- reliability analysis
- failure mode and effects analysis (FMEA)
- function analysis
- Taguchi methods
- quality function deployment (QFD) (Lochner and Matar, 1990; Clausing, 1997).

Most of these techniques focus on ensuring that a developed product fully satisfies customer requirements. For example, TQM focuses on the management aspects of quality (Hellard, 1993). Reliability analysis addresses the quality of a product with respect to its proper operation over the anticipated life. FMEA focuses on the systematic identification of the potential product or process failures (Lochner and Matar, 1990). Taguchi methods, developed by Dr Genichi Taguchi, deal with the robust design of products with respect to product concept selection, parameter optimisation and minimisation of variations in product performance (Fowlkes and Creveling, 1995). However, QFD is associated mostly with encapsulating the 'voice of the customer' in product development (Akao, 1990a, 1990b; Dean, 1992). Therefore, it provides an appropriate framework for investigating the processing of customer requirements in manufacturing. Its close association with the concurrent engineering philosophy (Dean, 1992; Clausing, 1997; Vilela and Cheng, 1997), a concept that is considered vital to the integration of the construction process, further suggests that it can also provide a good basis for the establishment of client requirements in construction.

3.4 Quality function deployment

Quality function deployment (QFD), which originated in Japan in the late 1960s, was developed to design quality into a product (Hauser and Clausing, 1988; Dean, 1992; Akao, 1997). It is defined as:

- a technique to convert user quality requirements into counterpart characteristics in order to determine design quality for the finished product (Akao, 1990a)
- a system for designing a product or service based on customer demands and involving all members of the producer or supplier organisation (Maddux *et al.*, 1991)
- a planning process that helps a company take the 'voice of the customer' into the company's product and manufacturing planning (Day, 1993)
- a matrix-based methodology for translating the customers' required quality characteristics into appropriate product or service features (Ranky, 1994)
- a systematic method of collecting input from all sources of significance to a project and integrating these into a coherent plan

for the whole organisation to follow in fulfilling the need (Davis, 1995)

- a market-driven technique to aid the design and development of products, processes and supporting services to meet or extend customers' needs and expectations (Johnston and Burrows, 1995).

3.4.1   QFD methodology

In QFD, customers' demands are converted into 'quality characteristics'. The design quality for the finished product is developed by systematically deploying the relationships between the demands and the quality characteristics, starting with the quality of each functional component and extending the deployment to the quality of each part and process (Akao, 1990b). This is accomplished through the use of:

- multidisciplinary teams in defining customer requirements
- charts and matrices to propagate critical customer wants throughout the product lifecycle
- the assignment of numeric values to qualitative levels of importance of customer requirements (Mitsufuji and Uchida, 1990; Sivaloganathan and Evbuomwan, 1997).

The overall QFD process comprises four phases (Figure 3.1). Phase 1 (product planning) deals with the translation of customer requirements into product measures (design requirements). It is also referred to as the 'house of quality' (Hauser, 1993). Phase 2 (parts deployment) translates the key product measures from phase one into parts characteristics. In phase 3 (process planning), key parts characteristics are translated into manufacturing process characteristics. In phase 4 (production planning), the manufacturing process characteristics are translated into manufacturing process controls (Halblieb *et al.*, 1993; Evbuomwan, 1994).

3.4.2   The 'house of quality'

The 'house of quality' matrix (Phase 1 of the QFD process — see Figure 3.1) is used to understand the 'voice of the customer' and to translate it into the 'voice of the designer' (Hauser and Clausing, 1988; Hauser, 1993;

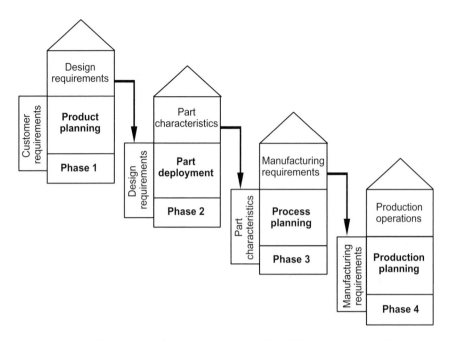

Figure 3.1. The four stages of the QFD process (adapted from Davis, 1995)

Evbuomwan, 1994). Figure 3.2 shows the basic features of the 'house of quality'. It contains nine 'rooms' or blocks, which represent different planning activities (Evbuomwan, 1994). The processes involved in 'building' the 'house of quality' have been analysed and are presented in Table 3.1.

3.4.3 Application and benefits of QFD

QFD has been used in a wide range of activities (Hauser, 1993; Halblieb *et al.*, 1993; Lockamy III and Khurana, 1995; Gustafsson *et al.*, 1997), particularly during requirements analysis for *product improvement* (e.g. when design engineering changes are to be brought about in the next generation of the product). The use of QFD for generating entirely new product ideas has been very limited. However, various benefits are associated with its use. These include:

- the utilisation of the collective knowledge of management in capturing and bringing the 'voice of the customer' into the

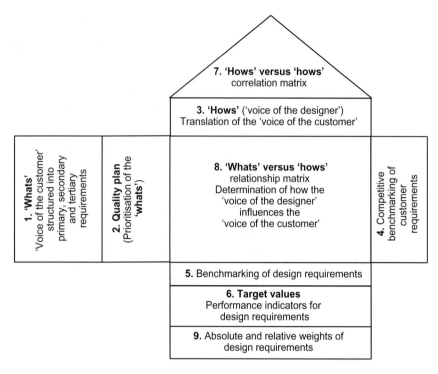

Figure 3.2. 'House of quality' chart (adapted from Evbuomwan, 1994)

production organisation (Maddux *et al.*, 1991; Tran and Sherif, 1995; Johnston and Burrows, 1995)

- the enhancement of communication through the use of procedures and processes that focus on the language of the customer, and the horizontal integration of functions (Hauser, 1993; Lockamy III and Khurana, 1995)
- the provision of a traceable path from the customer down to the most detailed processes, throughout each stage of the product development cycle (Ranky, 1994)
- the provision of a repository for product plans and specifications through simultaneous capture of customer and product requirements (Tran and Sherif, 1995)
- the provision of a simple strategic method for assessing the impact of changes to requirements, and resolving anomalies at the earliest stages of the project (Johnston and Burrows, 1995).

Table 3.1. Building the 'house of quality'

Step	Task	Description
1	Identify customer requirements ('voice of the customer' — 'whats')	Requirements identified in the language of the customer and structured into primary, secondary and tertiary requirements
		Primary requirements relate to the strategic needs of the product; secondary needs are decompositions of primary needs; tertiary needs are further decompositions of secondary needs
2	Prioritise customer requirements	Tertiary customer requirements are prioritised by taking into account the customers' rating, sales advantage, and quality target improvement factors (i.e. the ratio of the targeted rating by the customers to the current rating of a company's product from competitive benchmarking)
		Absolute importance rating of each tertiary requirement is the product of the ratings from the above three contributors
		Relative ratings of tertiary requirements are obtained by normalising the absolute values on a scale of 1 to 9
3	Identify technical features — 'hows' ('voice of the designer')	Measurable technical features (quality characteristics, design requirements or product specifications) that will fulfil customer requirements are identified
		Design requirements, which should be dependent variables, are assigned physical measurement units that then become targets for the design team ('target values')
4–6	Benchmark customer, and design requirements	Compare the company's product or design and associated performance levels against those of other companies or competitors
		The aim is to modify the targets for the design requirements that satisfy the customer requirements and, hence, exceed competitors' designs

Table 3.1. continued

Step	Task	Description
7	Develop the correlation ('hows' versus 'hows') matrix	Check and/or quantify the possible interactions among the design attributes in order to identify areas of inherent conflicts between the design requirements
8	Develop the relationship ('whats' versus 'hows') matrix	Identified design requirements are matched to customer requirements to determine the relationship between them
		The strength of the relationship between the two is expressed by numbers (9, 3, 1 and 0, for strong, medium, weak and no relationship, respectively) or symbols ($\odot$, $\bigcirc$, Δ and blank space)
9	Determine the absolute and relative weights of design requirements	Absolute weights of design requirements are calculated from the sum product of relative weights of tertiary customer requirements and the strength of the relationship between that requirement and a design requirement
		Relative weights are obtained by normalising the absolute values on a scale of 1 to 9 (or some other appropriate scale)

3.4.4   Limitations of QFD

Although QFD is beneficial to the product development process, there are limitations to its use. For example, it has been observed that the effectiveness of QFD diminishes downstream (i.e. from stages 2 to 4 — parts deployment to production planning — in Figure 3.1) in the product development process (Evbuomwan, 1994). It is also considered to be mainly quality based and does not specifically address cost, tools and technology, responsiveness, and organisational aspects in the same vein as it does quality. This, it is argued, makes QFD less likely to deal with complex products and conflicting requirements (Prasad, 1996). These limitations have led to various extensions to the basic QFD matrix and other concepts such as design function deployment (DFD) and concurrent function deployment (CFD) (Evbuomwan, 1994; Prasad, 1996). However, in spite of these limitations, which relate to the *overall* product development process, QFD appears to be a useful tool in defining and encapsulating the 'voice of the customer' in product design. This is probably why the 'house of quality' is the most familiar aspect of QFD (Hauser, 1993).

3.5 Other techniques for requirements processing in manufacturing

Other techniques that are used to determine customer requirements in manufacturing include:

- functional analysis (Miles, 1972; Clausing, 1997)
- people-oriented methodologies (Gause and Weinberg, 1989; Ulrich and Eppinger; 1995)
- the use of formal methods for specifying requirements (Lin *et al.,* 1996)
- modelling tools (Hasdogan, 1996)
- computer-based systems (Tseng and Jiao, 1998).

These techniques are generally aimed at the precise definition, representation and management of customer requirements in product development. These approaches include the following:

(*a*) Further clarification of established practices. Both the approach described by Ulrich and Eppinger (1995) and functional analysis (Clausing, 1997) provide added insight into the definition of design requirements or technical specifications (block 3 in Figure 3.2) in QFD.

(*b*) The use of first-order logic to formally describe and represent requirements that support a generic requirements management process in the engineering design domain (Lin *et al.,* 1996).

(*c*) The use and adoption of functional requirements patterns from past design efforts for requirements management in product definition. This is facilitated by a computerised database system that integrates customer and design information for reuse (Tseng and Jiao, 1998).

(*d*) The categorisation of requirements into functions, attributes, constraints, preferences and expectations (Table 3.2), as a means of removing ambiguities in their definition (Gause and Weinberg, 1989).

Table 3.2. Components of requirements (compiled from Gause and Weinberg, 1989)

Component	Meaning
Functions	These are defined as the 'whats' of a product: that is, a description of what the product is to accomplish. Functions are verbs, representing actions for which the product is the subject. There are generally three categories of functions: evident, hidden and frill. Evident functions are those to be performed in a manner that is as visible, or evident to the user as possible. Hidden functions are to be imperceptible to the user. Frill functions are those that the client would like, but not if they cost anything
Attributes	These are desired characteristics, or adjectives/adverbs that describe the features of a product. An attribute should generally complete a statement such as, 'The product should be...'. Attributes provide modifications for functions. For example, a function for a lift information device, such as 'display directory information', can be modified by the attribute 'reliability'
Constraints	A constraint is a mandatory condition placed on an attribute. It represents the boundaries of the solution space for a design that satisfies an attribute. If a constraint is relaxed, it increases the size of the solution space and, therefore, the number of potential solutions. On the other hand, if the constraint is tightened, the solution space and the potential solutions are decreased
Preferences	A preference is a desirable but optional condition placed on an attribute. Any final design solution that satisfies every constraint is an acceptable solution but some acceptable solutions might be preferable to others. Preferences enable the designer to compare acceptable solutions and choose better ones
Expectations	These provide the basis for client satisfaction because disappointment and delight are not usually a matter of delivery but of how well delivery matches the client's expectations. Identifying expectations is important because the perspectives of people (especially between client and designer) are different. It is also important to determine, early on in the product development process, whether client expectations can be matched by the technical capabilities of available technology or the designer

From the foregoing discussion, it is evident that the definition of customer requirements in product development involves a range of techniques and methods that are integrated into a set of defined activities. It is further observed that QFD can serve as a suitable framework for encapsulating the 'voice of the customer' in the product development process, if it is enhanced by other techniques. While these tools can be people-oriented or paper-based, the growing tendency is for formal specifications and computer-based systems to be used in the management of requirements. This is particularly evident in requirements engineering.

3.6 Requirements processing in requirements engineering

Requirements engineering is a branch of software engineering that deals with the functions and constraints of software systems (Zave, 1995). It deals with the formalisation of ideas, and with the agreement of various perspectives (Paredes and Fiadeiro, 1995). Requirements engineering is widely applied in the development of software systems for telecommunications switches, data management in aircraft, command and control systems (e.g. weapon systems), and for power train control in the automotive industries (Stevens and Putlock, 1997). Its importance is based on the fact that incomplete, or inadequately defined, requirements are most often to blame for the failure of software development projects (Stevens and Martin, 1997).

3.6.1 Requirements management

The goal of requirements engineering is the effective management of requirements throughout the lifecycle of a software system. This is referred to as requirements management, defined as the process of creating, disseminating, maintaining and verifying requirements (Fiksel and Hayes-Roth, 1993). Requirements management ensures that customer wants are defined precisely, and that the solution efficiently meets those requirements (Stevens and Martin, 1997). It starts with the definition of what is required and culminates in the acceptance of the product against the requirements. The requirements management process consists of four main functions that are performed in an iterative fashion:

- requirements definition
- requirements analysis

- requirements tracking
- requirements verification (Ross and Schoman, 1977; Fiksel and Hayes-Roth, 1993).

These functions provide an insight into the processing of requirements in requirements engineering.

3.6.1.1   Requirements definition

This includes, but is not limited to, the problem analysis that yields a functional specification. It is a careful assessment of the needs that a system is to fulfil and involves context analysis (justification for a system), functional specification (what the system is to be) and design constraints (specifications of how the system is to be constructed) (Ross and Schoman, 1977).

3.6.1.2   Requirements analysis

This refers to the process of understanding and recording (or *representing*) in a clear form the requirements or needs to be met by the design and construction of a system (Freeman, 1980). It involves the interpretation of customer needs and deriving explicit requirements that can be understood and interpreted by people and/or computer programs. Requirements analysis results in *specifications* (Freeman, 1980) that are represented in documents and drawings, contextual data, flow-down relationships and computer executable languages (Fiksel and Hayes-Roth, 1993).

3.6.1.3   Requirements tracking

Requirements tracking, or traceability, involves the continuous interchange and negotiation within a project team regarding conflicting and changing objectives (Fiksel and Hayes-Roth, 1993). It also refers to the techniques used to represent relationships between requirements, and the design and implementation of a system (Ramesh *et al.*, 1995).

3.6.14   Requirements verification

This refers to the procedure for determining whether or not a product design complies with a designated set of requirements. This is accomplished either through human observation and sign-off, or through automated algorithmic methods (Fiksel and Hayes-Roth, 1993).

Table 3.3 provides a brief description of the various activities involved in requirements management.

3.6.2   Tools and techniques for requirements management

Requirements management in requirements engineering is mostly computer-based, and is facilitated by a range of tools for the analysis (definition, representation), tracking and verification of requirements. Table 3.4 provides a list of software tools that can be used for various requirement management functions.

Table 3.3.   Effective requirements management (after Fiksel and Hayes-Roth, 1993)

Activity	Description
Define requirements	Must enable efficient entry and updating of requirements information in a form that facilitates retrieval and comprehension by multiple users
Trace requirements	Must capture the relationship of detailed requirements to original customer needs
Avoid mistakes	Must ensure that all lifecycle requirements have been considered systematically as early as possible in the product development process
Evaluate requirements	Must check compliance status for selected requirements or groups of requirements, with a minimal time delay and redundant effort
Manage complexity	Must handle complex work breakdown structures involving large numbers of varied requirements for multiple subsystems that are assigned to different development activities or groups
Preserve history	Must compile a record of requirements evolution and design compliance, as well as rationales for changes introduced
Optimise design	Must ensure semantically that design conflicts, interactions, or trade-offs are detected, and that the best available knowledge is used to enhance design

Table 3.4. Software tools and applications in requirements management (compiled from Freeman, 1980; Fiksel and Hayes-Roth, 1993; Kott and Peasant, 1995; DOORS, 1997; Rational Rose, 1998)

Software category	Functions supported
General-purpose tools	
Text processors	Express and retrieve requirements in text form, including hypertext, outlining, and other aids
Spreadsheet tools	Track requirements (e.g. cost) based on arithmetic formulae, in some cases with automated links to design data
Database systems	Provide limited requirements storage, retrieval, tracking and report generation
Project management tools	Support management of complex projects, with schedule and resource tracking
Specialised tools	
Computer-aided engineering	Software and systems engineering, design expression, requirements consistency checking
Systems engineering tools	Requirements definition, decomposition, analysis, verification, and documentation (e.g. modelling languages, such as Unified Modelling Language (UML))
Quality management tools	Customer needs analysis, competitive benchmarking, design trade-offs
Traceability tools	Requirements documentation, flowdown, allocation and tracking
Commercial and specific software applications	
DOORS (Dynamic Object Oriented Requirements System)	Commercial software for requirements management. Utilises an object-oriented database to create structured requirements documents and provide automated links to systems design and implementation outputs
RequisitePro	Commercial, Windows-based tool for requirements management. Organises requirements in a repository and provides traceability and change management throughout project lifecycle
Requirement Specification Language	Description and encoding of requirements in formal statements (such as the example in Figure 3.3) and storage in a shared database (also known as Problem Statement Langauge (PSL))

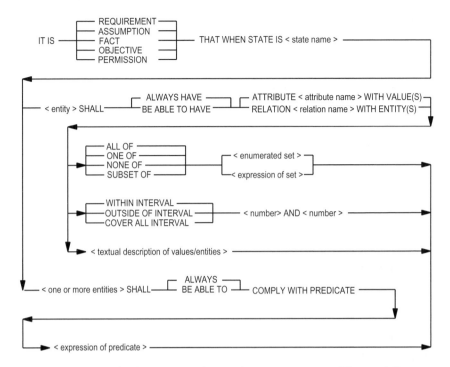

Figure 3.3. Generalised structure of a requirement statement (Kott and Peasant, 1995)

The following observations can be made about requirements processing in requirements engineering:

- the focus is on the management of requirements throughout the entire development process and goes beyond merely establishing the 'voice of the customer'
- the tools and techniques are computer-based, as the whole process of requirements management is geared towards automation
- formal and structured methods, including specification languages, are used in the definition and representation (or translation) of requirements
- database systems (relational or otherwise) play a vital role in the management of requirements.

Approaches to the application of these lessons from requirements engineering, as well as those from manufacturing, to the construction industry are now discussed.

3.7 Application to construction

The establishment of client requirements in construction projects should be based on a framework that satisfies the objectives defined in Chapter 1 (and reproduced in Section 3.2). The application of requirements processing techniques from manufacturing and requirements engineering to construction is, therefore, with respect to the requirements for establishing the 'voice of the client'.

3.7.1 Application of requirements processing techniques to construction

The extent to which the requirements for establishing the 'voice' of clients are supported by the techniques for requirements processing in manufacturing and requirements engineering is summarised in Table 3.5.

It is evident that these tools and techniques can facilitate, in principle at least, the processing of client requirements on construction projects. In particular, the QFD technique can contribute to the precise definition of requirements, representation in a solution-neutral format, and facilitate the traceability and correlation of requirements. This view is supported by various attempts to apply QFD principles to construction, which include:

- the design of factory-manufactured housing (Shiino and Nishihara, 1990)
- the renovation of a computer workroom facility (Mallon and Mulligan, 1993)
- the design of the layout of a restaurant and the structural elements of an industrial building (Huovila *et al.*, 1997)
- the determination of design characteristics for the internal layout of a building complex (Serpell and Wagner, 1997)
- the processing of client requirements for a building project (Kamara *et al.*, 1999).

However, most of these attempts were undertaken within the context of conventional approaches to the construction process, which are

Table 3.5. Possible support tools and techniques for client requirements processing

Need for client requirements processing	Possible support tools and techniques to achieve need
Clear and unambiguous to minimise/eliminate confusion and to facilitate verification and management of requirements	People-oriented techniques (e.g. interviews and brainstorming exercises), formal methods and templates, specification languages, structuring and decomposition of requirements into a hierarchy (primary, secondary, tertiary) as in QFD, or into different parts (functions, attributes, constraints, etc.)
	QFD correlation matrix (or other matrix-based tool), decomposition of requirements, knowledge-based inference engines, multi-user relational database systems
Representation in solution-neutral format and in a manner that facilitates understanding from different perspectives	Formal methods and templates, specification languages, effective translation/mapping of client requirements into design attributes as in QFD, relevant international standards (e.g. for representing user-requirements, data representation and exchange, etc.)
Comprehensive (incorporating different perspectives and lifecycle issues)	Decision support tools, such as expert and knowledge-based systems; multi-user database systems that allow the input of clients; people-oriented tools
Adequate framework to ensure required outputs are delivered	Structured processes and varied computer-based (and/or information) tools and technologies
Computer based	Use of varied computer-based tools and technologies (e.g. relational database and spreadsheet packages); customisation of available commercial software packages

considered to produce less than optimal results. They also do not address the organisational complexities that affect the processing of client requirements. For example, potential 'users' of facilities are likened to potential 'customers' of 'off the shelf' products in manufacturing. While the 'clients' of speculative developers in construction approximate to 'customers' of 'off the shelf' manufactured products, constructed facilities are usually purchased before they are designed or built (Kometa and Olomolaiye, 1997).

3.7.1.1   *The need for customisation*

The inadequacies of various attempts to implement QFD in construction suggest that the tools and techniques for requirements processing and management in manufacturing and requirements engineering need to be specifically adapted to suit the construction process. For example, in developing the 'quality plan' ('whats') (i.e. the prioritisation of client requirements), the approach used in manufacturing should be modified when applying QFD to construction (Kamara *et al.*, 1999). In manufacturing, the calculation of the importance ratings (relative weights) for customer requirements is based on the *customer's importance rating*, the *improvement required* based on competition and other analyses, and *sales advantage* (Sivaloganathan and Evbuomwan, 1997). This is associated mostly with market surveys of customer demands and information on existing products. In construction, the products (e.g. bridges and roads) are made to order and factors such as 'sales advantage' and 'required improvements because of competition' do not usually apply, except in speculative house or office buildings and in the refurbishment of existing facilities. However, even in these cases, the client, as project initiator and representative of the 'user', provides the project team (product development team) with the requirements for the desired facility. Therefore, in developing the 'quality plan', different project and client types should be taken into consideration.

3.7.1.2   *The need for other tools and techniques*

Table 3.5 shows that other tools and techniques, particularly decision-making tools, need to be utilised to fully address the requirements for establishing client requirements on construction projects. The need to customise techniques, such as QFD, also requires the incorporation of various tools that will reflect the reality in construction. For example, a definitive method to structure client requirements within QFD is required. Other tools and techniques can include those that are already in use in construction, or which are applicable to the general manufacturing process, or other disciplines. It must be emphasised that, as a first step, the focus is on paper-based methods, which need to be sufficiently workable before computer implementation.

3.7.2 Additional tools and techniques for establishing client requirements

These include decision-making tools and those that will facilitate the structuring of client requirements, and the generation of design requirements (Kamara *et al.*, 1998). Decision-making techniques are necessary to ensure that the perspectives and priorities of clients are incorporated fully in the design and construction process. This can be achieved through the use of techniques such as the analytic hierarchy process (AHP), criteria weighting (CW) and the weighted score model (WSM).

3.7.2.1 Analytic hierarchy process

The analytic hierarchy process (AHP) is a multicriteria decision-making technique, which was developed by Thomas L. Saaty in the early 1970s (Zahedi, 1986; Saaty, 1990). It is a systematic procedure for representing the elements of any problem. It organises the basic rationality by breaking down the problem into its smaller constituent parts and then uses pair-wise comparison judgements to develop priorities in each hierarchy (Saaty, 1982). Using AHP in problem-solving involves four steps (Zahedi, 1986):

1. Setting up a decision hierarchy of the problem by breaking down the decision problem into a hierarchy of interrelated decision elements, as in Figure 3.4, which illustrates a possible decision hierarchy for buying the 'best new house'.
2. The collection of input data by pair-wise comparisons of decision elements of one level that contribute to achieving the objective(s) of the next higher level (for example, the elements in level 2 of Figure 3.4 — price, monthly payment, and size and location — contribute to achieving the objective in level 1, that is, the best new house to buy).
3. Using an 'eigenvalue' method, which takes into consideration the pair-wise comparisons in step 2, to estimate the relative weights of decision elements.
4. Aggregating the relative weights of decision elements to arrive at a set of ratings for the decision alternatives (or outcomes) (level 3 in Figure 3.4).

AHP has been applied to a wide range of problems, including:

- architectural design (Saaty and Beltran, 1980)
- project selection and resource allocation (Zahedi, 1986)

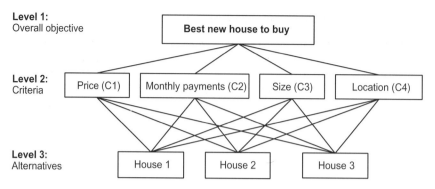

Figure 3.4. *Hierarchy of decision levels in AHP (adapted from Saaty, 1982)*

- sheet bending design (Lin and Shieh, 1995)
- assessing success factors for implementing concurrent engineering in a plastic products industry (Tummala *et al.*, 1996)
- the selection of vendors for IT outsourcing decisions (Akomode *et al.*, 1998).

Some aspects of the technique, especially pair-wise comparisons, can be used to determine the relative weights of the requirements with respect to the different perspectives within the client body. However, the choice of alternatives (step 4 in the methodology), which can imply the choice of a suitable design alternative to satisfy a requirement, will negate the need to express requirements in a solution-neutral format.

3.7.2.2 *Criteria weighting*

Criteria weighting (CW) is a technique, similar to AHP, that is used for decision-making using economic and non-economic criteria. It is part of the suite of techniques used in value management and also uses a system of pair-wise comparisons to clarify and rank a client's objectives, as well as provide guidance for design decisions (ICE, 1996b). The procedure used in this technique to assign weights to a set of requirements (column 2 in Table 3.6) is as follows:

1. A notation (a letter) is assigned to each requirement (column 1 in Table 3.6).
2. Each requirement is compared with every other requirement in turn (pair-wise comparison) using a criteria-scoring matrix (Figure 3.5). In rating comparisons, there are four preferences to

Table 3.6. Raw scores and importance weights for requirements (after ICE, 1996b)

Notation (1)	Requirement (2)	Raw score (3)	Relative weight (4)
A	Energy reduction	10	4·76
B	Cost of maintenance	9	4·28
C	Redesign time/cost	14	6·67
D	Performance	21	10·00
E	Aesthetics	5	2·38
F	Ease to erect	7	3·33
G	Salvage value	1	0·48
H	Impact on building cost	7	3·33

choose from: major, medium, minor and no preference. These have been assigned scores of 4, 3, 2 and 1, respectively. For example, in Figure 3.5, because requirement A is considered to be of minor preference to requirement C, the comparison between A and C is given as A–2 in column C. Where there is no preference, the score is written down in a letter–letter format (e.g. A–B in column B of Figure 3.5), and each letter is allocated a score of 1.

3. With the matrix completed, the next step is to calculate the raw score (absolute weight, AW_r) for each requirement. This is given by:

$$AW_{ri} = \Sigma W_i \qquad (1)$$

	B	C	D	E	F	G	H
A	A–B	A–2	D–4	A–3	F–2	A–3	A–H
B		B–3	D–3	B–E	B–2	B–G	B–H
C			C–2	C–3	C–3	C–4	C–2
D				D–4	D–3	D–4	D–3
E					E–F	E–3	G–H
F						F–3	F–H
G							H–3

Importance:
4 = Major preference
3 = Medium preference
2 = Minor preference
1 = Slight, no preference

Figure 3.5. Criteria scoring matrix for requirements in Table 3.6 (after ICE, 1996b)

where W_i is the weighting for the ith requirement (i = A, B,..., I in this case). The weighting for each requirement is obtained by adding the numbers following that requirement in the criteria scoring matrix (Figure 3.5). For example, the raw score for requirement A is 10 (i.e. 1 + 2 + 3 + 3 + 1). This is the raw score (absolute weight) that is included in column 3 of Table 4.7. The relative weight (RW_{ri}) of each requirement is derived by setting the highest requirement weight as 10 and, using proportionality, calculating the weight for each of the remaining requirements. Thus:

$$RW_{ri} = \left(\frac{AW_{ri}}{AW_{max}} \right) \times 10 \qquad (2)$$

Calculated values are given in column 4 of Table 3.6.

3.7.2.3 Weighted score model

The weighted score model (WSM) combines quantitative and qualitative measures as an aid to operational decision-making, and enables multiple criteria (aspects of organisational importance) to be taken into account (Griffith and Headley, 1997). It can be used to decide on the best house to buy (Figure 3.4) based on the relative score of each house with respect to the defined criteria (price, monthly payment, size and location). This can be done as follows:

1. Determine the relative importance of each criterion (using either subjective judgement, pair-wise comparisons or some other means) (column 2 in Table 3.7).
2. Determine how each house rates against each criterion (columns 3–5 in Table 3.7).
3. Calculate the weighted score for each house by taking the sum product of the relative importance of each criterion and the rating of the house on that criterion (i.e. column 2 multiplied by each of columns 3, 4, and 5 in Table 3.7). The sum product represents the absolute weight for each house. Relative weights can be calculated using the method described for criteria weighting.

The WSM is similar to the method for determining the absolute weight of design requirements used in QFD. It is also similar to the AHP method, except that in the AHP method, matrix algebra is used to determine the relative weights of identified criteria.

Table 3.7. Using weighted score model to decide on buying a house

Criteria	Relative weight	House 1	House 2	House 3
(1)	(2)	(3)	(4)	(5)
Price	3	3	2	3
Monthly payment	4	2	5	1
Size	1	4	1	4
Location	2	1	2	4
Sum product (absolute weight of house)		23	31	25
Relative weights (optional)				

3.7.2.4 Miscellaneous tools and techniques

Value tree analysis This is used in value engineering to decompose requirements (ICE, 1996b). This technique, which is similar to the function analysis system technique (FAST), uses the question 'how?' in decomposing functions from general to specific, and the question 'why?' to check the validity of the decomposition from specific to general. Value tree analysis can be used to structure client requirements into a hierarchy from the general (strategic) to the specific (i.e. into primary, secondary and tertiary requirements). The suggestion by Ulrich and Eppinger (1995) that the structuring of requirements be considered as a process of assigning groups to a cluster of similar requirements can also be combined with value tree analysis to provide an effective process of structuring requirements.

International standards These include ISO 6242: 1-3, 1992 (the specification of user requirements in building construction) (ISO, 1992), which specify the representation of user requirements and can also be used in client requirements processing. When used in conjunction with the QFD matrix, these standards are useful in translating the 'voice of the client' into the 'voice of the designer'.

Elicitation techniques This covers tools and techniques such as interviews, group discussions and departmental meetings, which are

Table 3.8. Specific tools for client requirements processing

Client requirements processing requirements	Specific tools and techniques	Rationale
Clear and unambiguous to minimise/eliminate confusion and to facilitate verification and management of requirements	Elicitation techniques (e.g. interviews, brainstorming exercises) depending on the type of project and client	The use of interviews and meetings to elicit requirements is already practised in construction
	Template for eliciting/documenting requirements	Use of a template will ensure completeness of information
	Value tree analysis/ function analysis to structure and group requirements	Value tree analysis will facilitate a better understanding of requirements among those involved in defining them
	A multidisciplinary requirements processing team (RPT)	The RPT will utilise the tools and techniques to define requirements
	QFD relationship matrix and a relational database for storing and manipulating structured requirements	Use of a matrix and a relational database can make it easy to trace relationships between requirements
Representation in solution-neutral format and in a manner that facilitates understanding from different perspectives	Semi-formal template and international standards (e.g. ISO, 1992) to assist in the generation of design requirements	The ISO (1992) provide standard definitions of user requirements. A semi-formal template will provide flexibility and ensure that generated design requirements are solution-neutral
	QFD relationship matrix to effectively map client requirements to design requirements	QFD matrix is suitable for mapping client requirements to design requirements

Table 3.8. continued

Client requirements processing requirements	Specific tools and techniques	Rationale
Comprehensive (incorporating different perspectives and lifecycle issues)	Template to identify and reflect the views of interest group within the client	Template will ensure that all interest groups are represented
	Criteria weighting (CW) and weighted score model (WSM)	Combining CW and WSM will ensure that client requirements can be prioritised with respect to the level of importance each interest group places on that requirement
Adequate framework to ensure required outputs are delivered	Modelling tools such as IDEF-0 and EXPRESS-G	Process and information/ data models will ensure that a defined process is followed; also helps in determining the kind of information to look for
Computer-based	Relational database	A database will facilitate the storage of information, which can be used in other, integrated applications
	Spreadsheet packages	Spreadsheets will facilitate calculations and matrix management

already in use for the elicitation of client requirements in the construction industry.

Other decision-making techniques These may include decision trees (a method closely associated with knowledge-based systems) (Gause and Weinberg, 1989; Griffith and Headley, 1997) and the Delphic hierarchy process (DHP), a hybrid method that combines the DHP method and the

AHP method (Khorramshahgol and Moustakis, 1988). The DHP method is a systematic procedure for evoking expert opinion through the use of statistical group response and controlled feedback.

3.7.3 Specific tools and techniques for client requirements processing

A review of the specific tools and techniques to support the establishment of client requirements on construction projects has been conducted and the results are presented in Table 3.8. Although these tools are varied, they are organised around the QFD technique for encapsulating the 'voice of the customer' in the product development process. The effective utilisation of these tools, however, can be done best in an integrated framework or model, which clearly describes the process involved in defining, analysing and translating client requirements into solution-neutral specifications. The development of a model for client requirements processing can also facilitate its implementation in a computer environment, and this is the subject of the next chapter.

Chapter 4

Methodology for client requirements processing

4.1 Overview of Chapter 4

This chapter describes the methodology for capturing client requirements in construction projects. This methodology, which is encapsulated in a client requirements processing model (CRPM), is designed to satisfy the goals for client requirements processing set out in Chapter 1, and utilises the tools identified in Chapter 3.

4.2 Evolution and development of the model

The client requirements processing model (hereinafter referred to as 'the model' or CRPM) is the representation of the proposed framework for establishing client requirements on construction projects. It describes the functions or activities that need to be undertaken, as well as the tools and techniques required, to effectively define, analyse and translate client requirements into solution-neutral design specifications.

4.2.1 Evolution of the model

The evolution of the CRPM was based on the need for an effective mechanism for the establishment of client requirements in construction, and the opportunities that exist, both within the industry and in other disciplines, to create such a framework for processing client requirements. Some of these opportunities included the following:

(*a*)   The recognition that improvements to the briefing process are vital, and that structured methods can enhance the briefing process (see Chapter 2).

(*b*)   Changing practices within the construction industry with respect to the increasing importance of project and/or construction managers in design and build, and management contracting. The role of project managers, who are not necessarily design-oriented, as leaders of the construction process, provides the opportunity for briefing (processing of requirements) to be approached differently from the usual practice of using design to clarify the client's problem.

(*c*)   The provision of separate briefing services to clients by some consulting firms is also another opportunity to introduce alternative approaches to the processing of client requirements, which will not be constrained by the pressures of design targets when briefing is combined with design.

(*d*)   Developments in manufacturing and requirements engineering in the effective processing and management of customer and system requirements, provide opportunities for incorporating similar tools and techniques, particularly QFD, in the processing of construction clients' requirements. The significance of this strategy is underscored by the fact that there are already precedents in applying manufacturing concepts to good effect in construction.

The established need for an improved framework for processing client requirements provided the *justification* for the CRPM. The opportunities, on the other hand, provided *ideas* for its development.

4.2.2   Conceptual development of the model

The CRPM is based on certain assumptions and its development was influenced by the requirements for a new structured approach to establishing client requirements on construction projects.

4.2.2.1   Assumptions

In the development of the CRPM, it was assumed that:

- there are always interest groups who influence, or are affected by, the acquisition, operation and existence of a facility; these groups can be within and/or outside the client body

- although the decision to build is usually made by top management (in the case of business clients), and is based on criteria (e.g. economic factors) that do not necessarily have to do with users (Kometa and Olomolaiye, 1997), the views of other interest groups, particularly end-users (both within and outside the client organisation) will be taken into account in defining client requirements.

4.2.2.2   Nature of the model

The CRPM is a novel, structured methodology for establishing client requirements on construction projects. Since the focus is on client requirements, it is important to restate here the definition of the terms 'client' and 'requirements' within the context of this book. The client is considered to represent the interests and views of the initiator of a project, as well as other parties (e.g. users and pressure groups) who influence, or are affected by, the acquisition, operation and existence of a constructed facility. These groups (especially users) are usually crucial to the success of a project but, since they are not in a direct contractual relationship with the suppliers of the facility (i.e. the construction industry), their interests may not necessarily be taken into consideration; especially when they are external to the client organisation.

Requirements are defined as the vivid description of the facility that satisfies the business need of the project initiator. The requirements of the client, therefore, include those of the project promoter as well as the views of other interest groups who he or she represents. Furthermore, it should be emphasised that client requirements are distinct from, and are a subset of, project requirements. To ensure continued focus on the client, the focus of the methodology being developed is on the requirements of the client and not on other project requirements (e.g. site conditions), which can either serve as constraints to, or opportunities for, satisfying client requirements.

4.2.2.3   The perspectives of the model

The framework for establishing client requirements can be considered as a 'system', which is defined as 'an interrelated set of objects or elements which are viewed as a whole and designed to achieve a purpose' (Britton and Doake, 1996). A system may be defined by the various perspectives, which include functional, informational and behavioural (Chung, 1989). The functional perspective defines the functions, which transform inputs into outputs, and the flows of data, which define the interrelations, between the functions of the system. The information perspective graphically illustrates the facts about the system, its definition of relevant information and their relationships. It is used to define the information flow and data requirements of a system. The behavioural perspective defines the different behavioural states (dynamic characteristics) of a system and the events that cause the transition from one state to the next. The CRPM is defined with respect to the functional and informational perspectives. It was not considered necessary to include a behavioural perspective because the establishment of client requirements is more dependent on information flows and the translation of such information from one form to another (input–output), rather than on 'time'. The issue of 'time' is more relevant to the management of requirements over the project lifecycle, and is outside the scope of this book.

4.2.2.4   *The process of developing the model*

The development of the CRPM involved an iterative process, which included a detailed study of QFD, the technique on which the model is generally based. There were also reviews and feedback by various academics and researchers, and detailed analysis and discussion with construction industry practitioners, many of whom provided assistance in evaluating the model.

4.3   The client requirements processing model

The CRPM is based on quality function deployment (QFD). The procedure for deploying the 'voice of the customer' using the QFD 'house of quality' was discussed in Chapter 3, but is summarised here for easy reference. It involves the following steps:

1. Identify customer requirements ('voice of the customer').
2. Prioritise customer requirements.
3. Identify technical features (design requirements/attributes).
4. Benchmark customer/design requirements (target values).
5. Develop correlation and relationship matrices.
6. Determine the absolute and relative weights of design requirements.

The CRPM was developed from the viewpoint of a project manager (or other professional) who has oversight over the processing of client requirements as well as other aspects of the project. This is because a person (or firm) in this capacity is in a position to understand all the interrelationships between the different tasks involved. The viewpoint of a project manager, therefore, represents a reasonably comprehensive view of the activities involved in client requirements processing. The key features of the model are presented in the subsequent subsections.

4.3.1   *Representation of the model*

The functional perspective of the CRPM is described using the IDEF-0 (Integration Definition level 0) notation for functional modelling (IDEF, 1993). An IDEF-0 model is a graphic representation of a system or subject that is developed for a specific purpose and from a selected viewpoint. IDEF-0 models are composed of three types of information: graphic diagrams, text and glossary, which are cross-referenced to each other. The graphic diagram is the major component of an IDEF-0 model, containing boxes, arrows, box/arrow interconnections and associated relationships. A box represents a major function of a subject. These functions (described using verbs or verb phrases) are decomposed into more detailed diagrams, until the subject is described at a level necessary to support the goals of the project. The top-level diagram in the IDEF-0 model provides the most general description of the subject and is followed by a series of child diagrams providing more detail about the subject. Arrows describe the things (i.e. data and objects) that constitute the system using nouns or noun phrases. The kinds of arrows (input, control, output, mechanism, etc.) used in IDEF-0 are illustrated in Figure 4.1.

4.3.2   *Main stages of the model*

The three main stages of the CRPM, illustrated in Figure 4.2, are:

- define client requirements
- analyse client requirements
- translate client requirements.

At the 'define requirements' stage, the interest groups represented by the client are identified and their requirements elicited. This function is further decomposed into three sub-activities. The 'analyse client requirements' function deals with the structuring and prioritisation of client requirements based on the relative importance interest groups

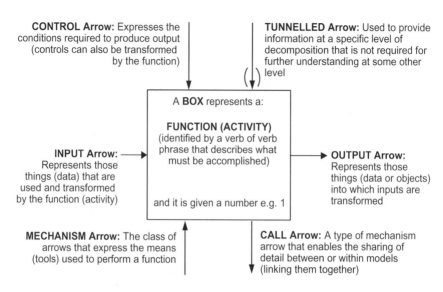

Figure 4.1. Basic concepts of the IDEF-0 notation

place on those requirements. This function is also decomposed into three sub-activities. The 'translate client requirements' function deals with the generation of design attributes, calculation of target values, translation of client requirements into design attributes, and the prioritisation of design attributes. This function is decomposed into four sub-activities. A detailed description of each stage in the CRPM is provided below.

4.3.2.1   Define client requirements

The 'define requirements' function is a decomposition of box 1 in the CRPM/A0 diagram (Figure 4.2) and it involves three activities:

- define project context
- identify client interest groups
- elicit client requirements.

Define project context   This activity deals basically with establishing and documenting basic facts about the project and the client. 'Client organisational factors' and 'project characteristics' provide the context for

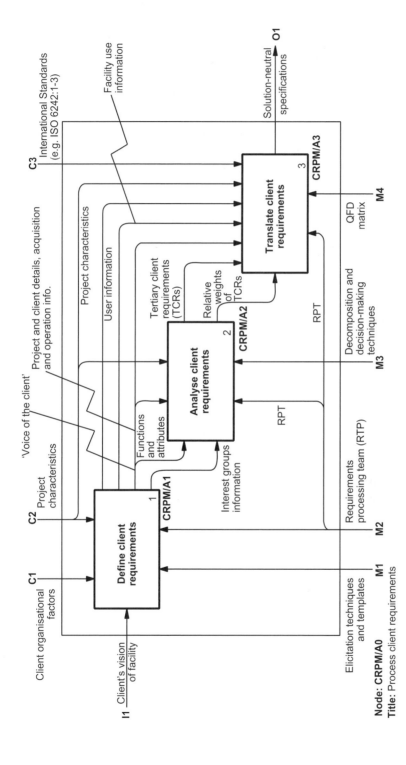

Figure 4.2. The three main stages of the CRPM

defining the details of the project (e.g. name and location) and those for the client (e.g. name and type of business). The mechanisms for this activity (and all sub-activities in the 'define client requirements' function) are the requirements processing team (RPT), and elicitation techniques and templates (e.g. questionnaires and interviews).

Identify client interest groups   This activity deals with identifying and describing the groups, which influence, or are affected by, the acquisition, operation/use and existence of the proposed facility. The client's vision for the facility provides the input for this activity, which is controlled by the project and client details, client organisational factors and the project characteristics.

Elicit client requirements   This activity converts the client's vision of the proposed facility into functions and attributes, acquisition and operation information, user information and facility use information. This activity is controlled by the interest groups information, the project and client details, client organisational factors and project characteristics. The project and client details, functions and attributes, and the acquisition and operation information, make up the 'voice of the client', which is one of the outputs of the 'define client requirements' activity.

4.3.2.2   Analyse client requirements

In this activity, which is a decomposition of box 2 in diagram CRPM/A0 (Figure 4.2), the requirements of the client are structured and prioritised. This is achieved through the following sub-activities:

- structure requirements
- prioritise interest groups
- prioritise tertiary requirements.

Structure requirements   In this activity, the functions and attributes of the facility are transformed into primary, secondary and tertiary requirements, using the RPT, and decomposition techniques (e.g. value tree analysis). The acquisition and operation information (which are also transformed by the structure requirements activity), project and client details, and project characteristics, provide the control for this activity.

Prioritise interest groups   This involves establishing the relative importance of different interest groups based on the information provided on them. This is done by the RPT using decision-making techniques such as criteria weighting. Controls for this activity are project characteristics, project and client information, and acquisition and operation information.

Prioritise tertiary requirements The prioritisation of tertiary requirements is based on the relative importance of each interest group and their weighting of each tertiary requirement. The RPT and decision-making techniques (weighted score model) are the means for carrying out this activity, which is controlled by the relative weights of interests groups, project characteristics, project and client details, and acquisition and operation information.

4.3.2.3 Translate client requirements

The 'translate client requirements' function, which is a decomposition of box 3 in diagram CRPM/A0 (Figure 4.2), involves the translation of client requirements into solution-neutral specifications. It consists of four sub-activities:

- generate design attributes
- determine target values for design attributes
- translate tertiary client requirements into design attributes
- prioritise design attributes.

Generate design attributes Design attributes are generated by the RPT. Tertiary requirements, project characteristics, international standards, and design attributes for similar facilities, provide the control for this activity.

Determine target values Target values are determined with respect to design attributes, project characteristics, use and user information, project and client details, acquisition and operation information for the facility, international standards, and target values for similar facilities. The RPT is the mechanism for this activity.

Translate tertiary requirements into design attributes Tertiary client requirements (TCRs) are associated with design attributes using the QFD 'house of quality' matrix and the experience of the RPT. The strength of the relationship between a requirement and a design attribute is represented by 9, 3, 1 or 0 for strong, medium, weak and no relationship, respectively. TCRs, project characteristics and the target values are the controls for this activity.

Prioritise design attributes The relative weights of TCRs and the strength of the relationship between TCRs and design attributes are used to calculate the relative weights of design attributes. The generated design attributes, target values, and relative weights for design attributes constitute the solution-neutral specifications, the overall output of the 'process client requirements' activity.

Figure 4.3 shows a flow diagram of all the activities in the model. A glossary of terms used is presented in Table 4.1.

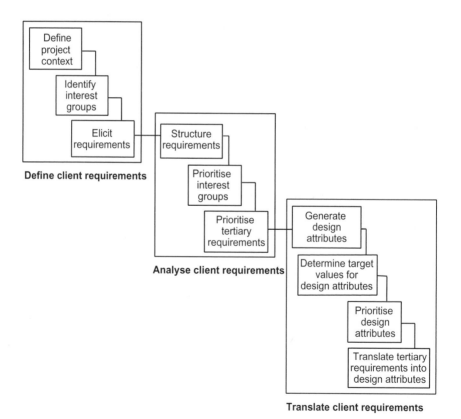

Figure 4.3. Flow diagram of all the activities in the CRPM

Table 4.1. Glossary of terms used in the CRPM

Term	Meaning
Acquisition information	Information relating to the acquisition of the facility (e.g. available budget, completion time and amount of risk the client is willing to take)
Attributes	Adjectives describing the proposed facility, normally preceded be the phrase, 'the facility should be...' (e.g. easy to sell, comfortable)
Client details	Specific details about the client that relate to the project (e.g. address, type of business, contact person for project, policies on space use)
Client organisational factors	The overall framework of the client organisation (e.g. decision-making process, organisational politics, ease of access to information, etc.)
Client's vision of facility	The perception of the client about the facility that will satisfy his or her business need (e.g. written notes, photograph of an existing building, a formal document, etc.)
Decision-making techniques	Techniques (e.g. criteria weighting) used to determine the priorities (absolute and relative weight) of an interest group, tertiary requirement or design attribute
Decomposition techniques	Techniques (e.g. value tree analysis) used to facilitate the structuring of client requirements into primary, secondary and tertiary requirements
Design attributes	Design requirements that relate to, and satisfy the requirements of, the client (e.g. gross floor area). They should be dependent variables within the design problem
Design attributes from similar facilities	Design attributes, which have been used in similar facilities and, therefore, can be adapted to the facility being proposed
Elicitation techniques/ templates	Techniques used to elicit information from the client and other interest groups (e.g. interviews, focus groups, seminars, questionnaires)
Facility use information	Information on the proposed use of the facility, i.e. activities that the facility will be used for (when performed, kind of equipment and furniture required)

Table 4.1. continued

Term	Meaning
Functions	Statements (verb–noun combinations) about what the facility should do. For example, provide space, facilitate communication and improve productivity
Interest groups information	Information on the interest groups (e.g. name and type of group, their influence in acquiring the facility, the likely effect of the facility on this group, etc.)
International standards	Standards that provide guidance on the expression of user requirements, as well as those that specify minimum/maximum values for design parameters
Operation information	Information on the proposed operation and management strategy, and level of technology, for the facility (e.g. centralised building management system)
Primary requirements	Statements that represent the most general requirements of the client. These can be decomposed into secondary and tertiary requirements
Project characteristics	These relate to the type of facility (e.g. building, road, bridge) and the nature of the project (e.g. whether it is a refurbishment, extension or 'new build')
Project details	Specific details about the project for which the requirements processing activity is a part (e.g. name, location, type of project, etc.)
QFD relational matrix	That part of the QFD 'house of quality' that deals with comparing the 'whats' (client requirements) and the 'hows' (design attributes)
Relative weights for design attributes	The relative importance of each design attribute
Relative weights of interest groups	The relative importance of each interest group
Relative weights of TCRs	The relative importance of each TCR
RPT	The team responsible for defining, analysing and translating client requirements into solution-neutral specifications

Table 4.1. continued

Term	Meaning
Secondary requirements	Decompositions of primary requirements which express the general requirements in greater detail
Solution-neutral specifications	A combination of design attributes, and the relative weights and target values for those attributes
Strength of relationships	A number indicating the strength of the relationship between a TCR and a design attribute
Target values	Specific values that define the solution space for design attributes (e.g. 5000 m^2 for gross floor area or 10% of gross floor area as circulation space)
Target values for similar facilities	Target values for similar facilities, or those that are considered to be best practice as a result of benchmarking
TCR	Decompositions of secondary requirements into greater levels of detail
User information	Information about the proposed users of a facility (e.g. type and size of users, and the activities they perform)
'Voice of the client'	Combination of: acquisition information, client details, facility attributes and functions, operation information, and project details. Expresses client wishes and expectations for the *product* (i.e. facility) and the *process* for its acquisition, operation and disposal

4.4   Informational perspective of the model

The informational perspective of the CRPM is represented using the EXPRESS-G graphical notation. An EXPRESS-G model is represented by three types of graphic symbols:

- definition symbols
- relationship symbols
- composition symbols.

Definition symbols (i.e. varying forms of rectangular boxes) are used to denote simple, constructed, defined, and entity data types, and schema declarations. Relationship symbols (lines) describe relationships which exist among the definitions. Relationships are bidirectional, but one of the two directions is emphasised, using an open circle in the emphasised direction. For example, in an entity-attribute relationship, the emphasised direction is towards the attribute. For inheritance relationships, the emphasised direction is toward the subtype. Composition symbols enable a diagram to be displayed on more than one page. When there is a relationship between definitions on separate pages, the relationship line on the two pages is terminated by an oval (rounded) box that contains a page number and a reference number. The page number is the number of the page where a referenced definition occurs. The reference number is used to distinguish between multiple references on a page. The composition symbol on the page where the reference originated contains the name of the referenced definition (ISO, 1994).

4.4.1   Informational representation of the CRPM

The informational representation of the CRPM defines the information required for defining, analysing and translating client requirements into solution-neutral design specifications. Table 4.2 provides a hierarchy of the types of information used in processing client requirements, and the groups to which they have been assigned for the purpose of the information model. The structure of these information types and the relationships are illustrated in Figures 4.4 to 4.7, which are an overview of the information model for the CRPM. The entities in the model, which are based on the information groupings in Table 4.2, and the relationships between these entities, are now described.

Client requirements, expressed as primary, secondary and tertiary requirements (with absolute and relative weights), describe the facility that satisfies the business need of the client. The requirements of the client consist of information relating to the characteristics of the client and the project (client/project characteristics), his or her business need (client business need), and the acquisition, operation and disposal of the facility (facility process). Client requirements are influenced by 'other sources of information' in the sense that a change in some standards (e.g. space standards or energy emission targets) might influence the decision by a client to commission the refurbishment of an existing building rather than embark on a new building project.

Table 4.2. List of information requirements for the CRPM

Information group	Basic information group contains
Client requirements ('voice of the client')	Primary requirements
	Secondary requirements
	Tertiary requirements (including relative weights)
	Client/project characteristics
	Client business need
	Facility process
Client business need	Facility use information
	User information
	Facility functions
	Facility attributes
Client/project characteristics	Client details
	Interest groups information
	Project details/characteristics
Facility process	Acquisition information
	Operation information
	Disposal information
Solution-neutral specifications	Design attributes
	Relative weights of design attributes
	Target values
Other sources of information	International standards
	Design attributes for similar facilities (benchmark information)
	Target values for similar facilities (benchmark information)

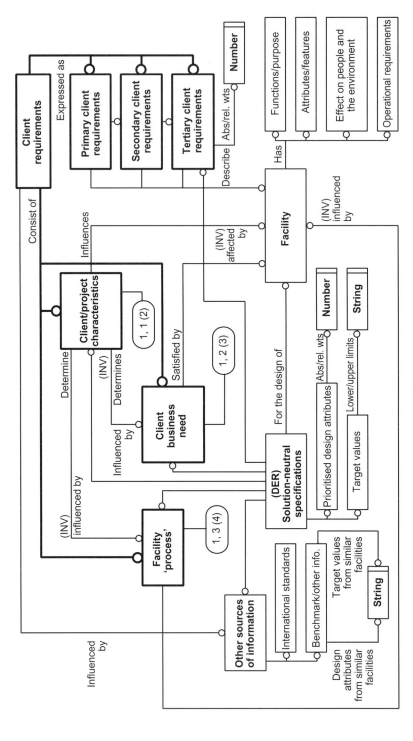

Figure 4.4. Complete entity-level diagram of the CRPM information model (page 1 of 4)

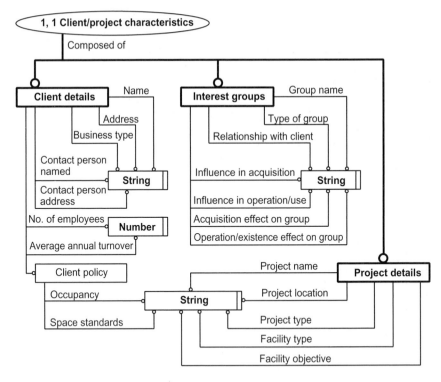

Figure 4.5. Complete entity-level diagram for the CRPM information model (page 2 of 4)

4.4.2   Details of the information model

Client/project characteristics include the nature of the client organisation and the project being considered. The client organisation determines the business need for a project. On the other hand, the business need (e.g. improved communication between two locations) influences the type of project (e.g. refurbishment) as well as the interest groups associated with the process and outcome of that project — the facility. The nature of the client organisation, and the kind of project, will also determine how the facility is procured, operated and disposed. For example, a client organisation with a substantial property portfolio can have property staff who are responsible for the acquisition of new property, unlike a one-off client who might require considerable assistance from outside consultants.

On the other hand, the facility process will have an influence on the organisation of the project. The attributes of the 'client/project characteristics' entity (Figure 4.5) are:

- client details (name, address, business type, contact person name, contact person address, number of employees, average annual turnover, and client policy on occupancy and space standards)
- interest groups (group name, type of group, relationship with client, group's influence in acquisition, influence in operation/use of facility, the effect of acquisition on the group and the effect on the group, of the operation/existence of the facility)
- project details (project name, project location, project type, facility type, and facility objective(s)).

The *client business need*, which has a relationship with *client/project characteristics*, is satisfied by the facility. The attributes of this entity (Figure 4.6) include the following:

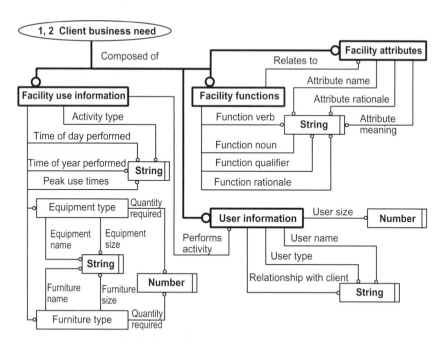

Figure 4.6. Complete entity-level diagram for the CRPM information model (page 3 of 4)

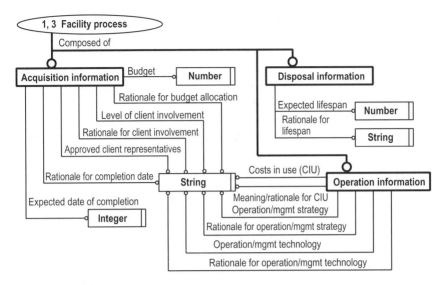

Figure 4.7. Complete entity-level diagram for the CRPM information model (page 4 of 4)

- facility use information (activity type, time of day performed, time of year performed, peak use times, and details of required equipment and furniture)
- user information (name, type, size, relationship with client, and activity performed)
- facility functions (function verb, noun, qualifier, and function rationale)
- facility attributes (attribute name, meaning, rationale, and associated function).

The user performs an activity (or activities), and facility attributes provide clarification for the functions of the facility.

The third component of the *client requirements* entity is *facility process* (i.e. information relating to the acquisition, operation and disposal of the facility) (Figure 4.4). Details of the *facility process* entity, which is influenced by the kind of facility the client requires (illustrated in Figure 4.7) include:

- acquisition information (available budget, rationale for budget allocation, level of client involvement, rationale for client involvement, approved client representatives, expected date of completion, and rationale for completion date)

- operation information (costs in use, meaning and rationale for costs in use, operation/management strategy, rationale for operation/management strategy, level of operation/management technology, and rationale for operation/management technology)
- disposal information (expected lifespan, and rationale for expected lifespan).

The attributes for *other sources of information* that influence *client requirements* (Figure 4.4) are international standards (including Codes of Practice) and benchmark/other information (based on existing or similar facilities, or other sources of information).

The entity, *solution-neutral specifications*, shown in Figure 4.4 is preceded by 'DER' (derived). This means that it is derived from 'other sources of information', 'facility 'process'', 'client/project characteristics', 'client business need' and 'tertiary client requirements'. Solution-neutral specifications, required for the design of the facility that satisfies the business need of the client, consist of prioritised design attributes (absolute and relative weights) and target values (lower and upper limits).

4.5 The CRPM and the objectives for establishing client requirements

The CRPM was developed to facilitate the establishment of client requirements in line with the objectives set out in Chapter 1. It represents a structured methodology and focuses on the description of the proposed facility that satisfies the business need of the client. The description is not based on the physical components of the facility (e.g. shape, materials, etc.) but on its functions, attributes, acquisition, operation, and effect on people and the environment. The manner in which the objectives for requirements processing are satisfied by the model is now discussed.

4.5.1 Clear and unambiguous requirements

The 'define client requirements' function provides for the precise establishment of the wishes and expectations of the client. From the informational perspective of the model, it is noted that information is solicited on the rationale for certain statements and desires of the client.

This assists the RPT to further clarify the real intentions of the client. It also ensures that the stated functions and attributes are not just 'wish lists' but are based on the descriptions that reflect the real (business) needs of the client. The structuring of requirements into primary, secondary and tertiary requirements further helps in clarifying and stating requirements in a concise and unambiguous manner. It also facilitates the tracing of requirements to the original intentions of the client (i.e. from strategic intentions to tactical statements that fulfil those intentions).

4.5.2   Representation in a solution-neutral format

The 'requirements definition' process focuses on the description of the proposed facility using terminology that is familiar to the client. The translation of requirements into design attributes using the QFD 'house of quality' matrix facilitates their presentation in design terms, and in a format that is independent of any design solution or materials specification. The use of a structured technique such as QFD ensures that design attributes adequately reflect the wishes and priorities of the client. The presentation of requirements in a solution-neutral format also ensures that the same requirements set is available to the various disciplines involved in a project, thereby facilitating their understanding from different perspectives.

4.5.3   Comprehensive requirements

The need to reflect the perspectives and priorities represented by the client is addressed by the information on interest groups, the prioritisation of these groups, and the prioritisation of tertiary requirements. The information on interest groups not only identifies these groups but also specifies how they influence, or are affected by, the acquisition, operation and existence of the facility. A systematic process, which incorporates the preferences of interest groups, is adopted for the prioritisation of client requirements. Furthermore, the use of formal decision-making techniques minimises bias in decision making but does not altogether remove the skills and experience of the RPT involved in the process. The CRPM also captures, early on in the process, information relating to the lifecycle of the facility (acquisition, operation and disposal information), which facilitates their incorporation into the design process.

4.5.4   Adequate framework

The CRPM provides an adequate framework, which addresses the complexities within the client body, clarifies the objectives and expectations of the client, and focuses exclusively on the requirements of the client. It also allows for the translation and presentation of client requirements in a format that engenders collaborative working and the development, verification and management of appropriate design and construction solutions that satisfy the needs of the client. The representation of the informational perspective using the EXPRESS-G notation will facilitate the implementation of the model in a computer environment. Information models described using EXPRESS-G are independent of any implementation context, thus allowing for flexibility in selecting computing environments that are compatible with activities/packages in the construction process. Examples of how the model can be implemented in practice are presented in the next chapter.

Chapter 5

Capturing client requirements with the client requirements processing model

5.1   Overview of Chapter 5

This chapter describes how client requirements are captured using the client requirements processing model (CRPM). It also specifies the context for its implementation with respect to the overall construction process and provides examples of how the model can be used in practice. Issues relating to the wider application of the methodology for different scenarios are also discussed.

5.2   General guidelines on the use of the CRPM

The CRPM is designed to facilitate the description of a proposed facility with respect to its functions, attributes, acquisition, operation, and effect on people and the environment. In line with recent moves towards the adoption of the performance-based building concept, the focus is on the elicitation of performance-related information rather than prescriptive details. The aim is to provide a link between the client's business need and technical design specifications, through the systematic mapping of strategic requirements to tactical solutions. While the model provides a structured methodology for achieving this, it is not intended to be a substitute for people and dialogue. Thus, the requirements processing team (RPT) is key to the utilisation of the CRPM. General guidelines on the implementation of the CRPM within the context of the overall construction process, and in specific projects, are presented below before some examples on the use of the model.

5.2.1 Implementation within the construction process

The context of the CRPM within the construction process is illustrated in Figure 5.1. The CRPM serves as the interface between the client's business needs and design requirements. It is performed *before* design (i.e. concept, scheme and detailed design). The outputs from the client requirements processing activity can facilitate a multidisciplinary design team to work collaboratively, and can serve as the basis for adopting a particular procurement/contract strategy. Comparing Figure 5.1 with Figure 2.3 (although the project frameworks are different), client requirements processing can be performed just before the appointment of a design team (i.e. at inception stage A), or this stage can involve parallel activities of processing client requirements and the setting up of the project organisation. However, a few points should be noted:

(*a*) The information generated by the client after the decision to build has been made (strategic requirements) can be varied depending on the type of client, project or facility being constructed. This information may also contain both prescriptive and performance related aspects of the proposed facility. These variations are accommodated by the 'define requirements' function of the model, which provides for the documentation of information in a consistent manner. Prescriptive information can be incorporated in the later stages of the model (e.g. in design attributes or in determining target values).

(*b*) In addition to the outputs of client requirements processing, other information, such as site conditions, and environmental and

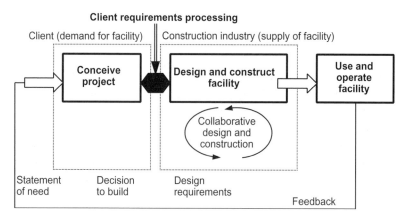

Figure 5.1. Context for the implementation of the CRPM

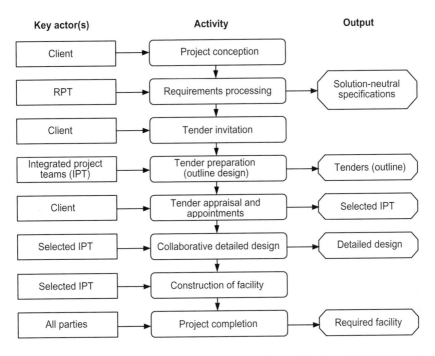

Figure 5.2. Possible procurement strategy for implementing the CRPM (adapted from Anumba and Evbuomwan, 1997)

regulatory requirements, are required to provide the context for the design of the facility. Although not indicated on the diagram, this information can be collected in parallel with the requirements processing activity.

5.2.2 Procurement/contract strategy for the CRPM

A possible procurement strategy for implementing the CRPM is illustrated in Figure 5.2. Following the conception of the project (corresponding to the conceive project stage of Figure 5.1), an RPT can be appointed to process the requirements of the client. This team is different from the project team and can include architects, project managers, engineers and facilities managers. The requirements processing activity can also be performed by firms, which offer a separate briefing service to clients. The solution-neutral specifications and other information, which result from requirements processing, can form the basis for tender invitations from integrated project teams (IPTs) (i.e. those with design and construction capabilities). The solution-neutral specifications also form the basis for collaborative outline and detailed designs. The role of IPTs can be fulfilled by design and build contractors who already have the organisation to offer design and construction services to clients. The CRPM can also be used in 'traditional' contracts, which are characterised by the separation of design and construction. In this case, design consultants (and not IPTs) will constitute the initial bidders for the project.

5.2.3 Implementation on specific projects

A key consideration in the use of the CRPM on specific projects is the kind of information that is elicited. In Section 1.3.2, three categories of client expectations were defined — basic, articulated and exciting needs. Although all three categories need to be satisfied in the constructed facility, elicitation and processing should generally focus on 'articulated' needs, except in cases where specific aspects of 'basic needs' (e.g. fire safety in a facility that is intended to handle flammable substances) are of particular importance to the proposed facility. The reason for this is that basic needs (e.g. fire integrity of buildings, structural stability, etc.) are usually linked with regulatory requirements and should be satisfied as a minimum. Therefore, it is helpful if these basic requirements are considered as 'constraints' to the articulated needs of clients (see Section 1.3.3). If they are combined with 'articulated needs', the prioritisation of client requirements will always be skewed in favour of basic needs. In the case of 'exciting' needs, these are 'extras' that exceed the client expectations. However, although they are not voiced, a thorough processing of 'articulated needs' will lead to the discovery of 'exciting' needs.

Other considerations in the use of the CRPM include the identification and prioritisation of 'interest groups', the structuring of client requirements and prioritisation of tertiary requirements, the generation of design attributes and the determination of target values (i.e. the design solution space for design attributes). These activities require value judgements to be made by members of the RPT. Therefore, it is necessary that members of the RPT are sufficiently knowledgeable of the construction process and the client organisation to make these judgements. It is recommended that the RPT is made up of representatives of the major disciplines involved in the lifecycle of a facility (e.g. architects, contractors, development managers, engineers, facilities managers, quantity surveyors, etc.) depending on the size and nature of the project. The following examples provide insights into how requirements are processed using the CRPM.

5.3   Illustrative examples on the use of the CRPM

Three examples of how the CRPM can be used to establish and process the requirements of clients are presented below. The first deals with a family house project. The second utilises the actual requirements of a university building project and describes how the CRPM could have been used on the project. The third example is a civil engineering road project and, like the second, uses an actual project (the Newbury Bypass Road Project) to illustrate the use of the CRPM.

5.3.1   Family house project

This is a hypothetical case of a client who wants to commission the construction of a country family house. The family is comprised of the husband (client), wife and a teenage son. The village in which the house is to be built has a very active parish council, which is very protective of the green open spaces in the area, and is very suspicious of any new developments.

5.3.1.1   Define client requirements

This first stage of the CRPM (see Figures 4.2 and 4.3) documents basic facts about the project and the client. The interest groups represented by the client are also identified and the requirements elicited. The outputs of the 'define client requirements' stage include:

- project and client details
- interest groups which influence, and are affected by, the acquisition, operation and disposal of the facility
- proposed use and users of the facility
- its functions and attributes
- information relating to the acquisition, operation and disposal of the facility.

Because this is a relatively small project, the outputs of the 'define client requirements' stage can be summarised and are shown in Table 5.1.

Table 5.1. Basic (hypothetical) details of the family house project

Kind of information	Details of information	
Project and client details	Project title:	Family house project (FHP)
	Type of project:	Building (new build)
	Client:	Mr F. Countryside
	Type of client:	Private individual
Facility use information	Kind of activities:	Family activities (sleeping, eating, cooking, etc.), entertainment of guests, storage of books (2000 volumes) and at least three cars, indoor exercise
	Time of use:	Mostly during summer months
User information	Year-round users (3):	Middle-aged (men or women) house servants
	Seasonal users (3):	Husband (late 40s), wife (mid-40s), son (late teens)
	Other users (up to 50):	Invited guests (late teens to middle age)
Interest groups	Users (including client); village parish council (very influential group)	
Functions of facility	The facility should provide adequate space for various family activities; provide privacy to its users	
Attributes of facility	The facility should be attractive, modern, comfortable, secure, easy to clean and maintain, inexpensive to operate, inoffensive to neighbours, flexible to allow future remodelling, easy to sell if necessary	
Acquisition, operation and disposal	Allowable budget:	250,000 pounds sterling
	Completion date:	Required in 12 months time
	Expected running costs:	Annual operating costs (cleaning, utilities, maintenance, etc.) not to exceed 15% of initial cost of construction
	Expected lifespan:	30 years

5.3.1.2   Requirements analysis

This involves the structuring of requirements and the prioritisation (ranking) of interest 'groups' and TCRs. The technique of value tree analysis (see Section 3.7.2.4) can be used to structure client requirements. Client requirements (i.e. functions and attributes of facility, etc.) are categorised into groups. The statement that best describes a group is a primary requirement (strategic requirements). This can either be an existing statement or an entirely new one. For example, from the functions and attributes in Table 5.1, 'attractive', 'modern' and 'inoffensive to neighbours' can be put into a group that describes the physical features of the house — 'attractive house' (Table 5.2). The question 'how?' (i.e. how can this requirement be implemented) is then used to decompose a strategic (higher-level) requirement into a tactical (lower-level) requirement. Moving backwards and asking the question 'why?' checks the decomposition (i.e. whether a lower-level requirement implements a higher-level one). Table 5.2 shows the structured requirements of the client. 'Attractive house' has been decomposed into 'blends with other buildings', 'aesthetically pleasing' and 'low running costs'. The three secondary requirements — 'attractive house',

Table 5.2. Structured requirements for the family house project

How? ⟶			⟵ Why?
Primary requirement	Secondary requirements	Tertiary requirements	Notation
A pleasant and entertaining family house	Attractive house	Blends with other buildings	R1
		Aesthetically pleasing	R2
		Low running costs	R3
	Cost effective	Easy to clean and maintain	R4
		Easy to remodel	R5
		Adequate space	R6
	Comfortable house	Adequate security	R7
		Minimal noise levels	R8

'cost-effective' and 'comfortable house' — are decompositions of the primary requirement, namely 'a pleasant and entertaining family house'. It should be noted that there is no 'right' result, as the structuring process depends on the RPT involved. What it achieves is a systematic way of distinguishing between strategic (primary) and tactical (secondary and tertiary) requirements, and a way of establishing relationships between them. The process is also iterative and the structuring process does not necessarily have to start from primary requirements.

Following the structuring of client requirements, interest groups are then prioritised to determine their level of importance. This can be done by pair-wise comparisons with other interest groups using criteria weighting (Section 3.7.2.2). The first step is to assign a notation (a letter) to each interest group (see Table 5.3). Each interest group is then compared with every other group in turn using the criteria-weighting matrix in Figure 5.3.

In rating comparisons, four preferences (major, medium, minor, no preference) are used, depending on the relative influence each interest 'group' has on the acquisition, use and operation of the facility. These preferences are assigned scores of 4, 3, 2, 1, respectively. For example, in Figure 5.3, because A (the husband) is considered to be of medium preference over C (the teenage son), the comparison between A and C is given as A–3 in column C. Where there is no preference, the score is written down in a letter–letter format (e.g. A–B, A–D, B–C, etc.) and each letter is allocated a score of 1.

With the matrix completed, the raw score (absolute weight, *AWS*) for each interest 'group' is then calculated. This is given by:

$$AWS_i = \Sigma WS_i \qquad\qquad (3)$$

Table 5.3. *Prioritisation of interest groups*

Notation	Interest group	Raw score (*AWS*)	Relative weight (*RWS*)
A	Mr F. Countryside (client)	10	9·0
B	Mrs F. Countryside (wife)	7	6·3
C	Teenage son	2	1·8
D	Parish council	6	5·4
E	House servants	4	3·6
F	Guests	5	4·5

	B	C	D	E	F
A	A–B	A–3	A–D	A–2	A–3
B		B–C	B–D	B–2	B–2
C			C–D	E–4	F–2
D				D–2	D–F
E					F–2

Importance:
4 = Major preference
3 = Medium preference
2 = Minor preference
1 = Slight, no preference

Figure 5.3. Pair-wise comparison of interest groups using criteria weighting matrix

where WS_i is the weighting for the ith group (= A, B,…,F, in this case). The weighting for each interest group is obtained by adding the numbers following that group in the criteria-weighting matrix (Figure 5.3). For example, the weighting for interest group A is 10 (i.e. $1+3+1+2+3$). This is the raw score (absolute weight), which is included in the third column of Table 5.3. Setting the highest weight (AWS_{max}) as 9 (or 10), the relative weight (RWS_i) of each group (listed in the fourth column of Table 5.3) can be calculated using the expression:

$$RWS_i = \left(\frac{AWS_i}{AWS_{max}} \right) \times 9 \qquad (4)$$

The relative weights for the TCRs can be determined using the relative weights of the interest 'groups', and the level of importance they place on each of the requirements. This is done using the matrix in Table 5.4. Interest groups and their relative weights are entered in the first two columns. Each group assigns a rating to each tertiary requirement. The rating is from 1 to 5 (1 being least important and 5 being the most important — or some other preferred scale). The absolute weight of each requirement (ABR_i) is given by:

$$ABR_i = \Sigma(RWS_i \times SR_i) \qquad (5)$$

where RWS_i is the relative weight of each stakeholder, and SR_i is the stakeholder rating for that requirement. For example, the absolute weight for requirement R3 (Table 5.4) is given by:

$$[(9 \times 5)+(6 \cdot 3 \times 2)+(1 \cdot 8 \times 2)+(5 \cdot 4 \times 1)+(3 \cdot 6 \times 2)+(4 \cdot 5 \times 1)] = 78 \cdot 3 \qquad (6)$$

The relative weights for each requirement is calculated using the same procedure as in the prioritisation of stakeholders described earlier. From Table 5.4, it can be seen that requirement R2 (aesthetically pleasing) has

Table 5.4. *Calculation of relative weights for tertiary client requirements*

Interest group	Tertiary requirements RWS	Blends with other buildings R1	Aesthetically pleasing R2	Low running costs R3	Easy to clean and maintain R4	Easy to remodel R5	Adequate space R6	Adequate security R7	Minimal noise levels R8
Mr F. Countryside	9	3	5	5	2	4	4	5	3
Mrs F. Countryside	6·3	2	5	2	3	3	5	5	5
Teenage son	1·8	2	3	2	2	3	4	4	5
Parish council	5·4	5	4	1	1	1	1	1	5
House servants	3·6	2	2	2	5	1	3	3	4
Guests	4·5	1	3	1	2	1	3	4	3
Absolute weights (ABR)		81·9	124·2	78·3	73	73·8	104·4	117·9	122·4
Relative weights (RVR)		5·9	9	5·7	5·3	5·4	7·6	8·5	8·9

Table 5.5. *Translation of tertiary requirements into design attributes (blank spaces in the matrix indicate no relationship)*

Design attributes	RWR	Energy efficiency D1	Impact sound transmission D2	Airborne sound transmission D3	Flexibility of spaces D4	Gross floor area D5	Quality of finish to external envelope D6	Number of access points D7	Fresh air supply D8	Level of internal finish D9
Tertiary requirements										
Blends with other buildings	5·9						9			
Aesthetically pleasing	9						9	1		
Low running costs	5·7	9			1	3	3	3	9	9
Easy to clean and maintain	5·3	1				3	9		1	9
Easy to remodel	5·4				9	9				3
Adequate space	7·6		3		3	9				
Adequate security	8·5						1	9		
Minimal noise levels	8·9		9	9		3	1			3
Absolute weights (AWD)		57	103	80	77	177	199	103	57	142
Relative weights (RWD)		2·6	4·7	3·6	3·5	8	9	4·6	2·6	6·4

the highest relative score of 9, while R4 (easy to clean and maintain) has the lowest rating, reflecting the lower rating of the interest group (house servants) that is most affected by this requirement.

5.3.1.3   Requirements translation

The translation of TCRs into solution-neutral specifications is done using the QFD 'house of quality' matrix in Table 5.5. Design attributes (technical specifications) are generated using the experience of the RPT, the requirements of the client, and various standards, such as ISO 6242 (ISO, 1992), for expressing user requirements in building construction (e.g. impact sound transmission, etc.). Measurable target values (design solution space) for each design attribute should also be determined, and the unit of measurement, where possible, specified. The information used to determine target values include facility use information (i.e. the kind of activities to be performed in the facility), user information (characteristics and physiological needs) and other external factors, such as international standards and benchmark information for similar facilities. The design attributes and indicative target values for the family house project are listed in Table 5.6. This is not an exhaustive list but it illustrates the nature of design attributes and their use in the CRPM. Details of the terms used and their measurement can be found in ISO 6242 (ISO, 1992) and *Building for energy efficiency* (CIC, 1997).

The relationships between tertiary requirements and design attributes are completed using 9, 3, 1 and 0 (or blank space) to denote strong, medium, weak and no relationship, respectively. For example, there is strong relationship between the requirement 'aesthetically pleasing' and the design attribute 'quality of finish to external envelope' (Table 5.5). Minimum noise levels have a very strong relationship with 'impact sound transmission' and 'airborne sound transmission'. These design attributes will influence the form of construction and materials that will affect/minimise the transmission of sound between rooms and for interior and exterior building elements (ISO, 1992). The absolute and relative weights for each design attribute are calculated using the same procedure for calculating the absolute and relative weight for tertiary requirements described earlier. Table 5.5 shows that the 'quality of finish to external envelope' has the highest relative weight, closely followed by 'gross floor area'. This means that these design attributes satisfy a greater proportion of the requirements of the client (as indicated by the greater frequency of relationships between tertiary requirements and design attributes), especially those requirements that are of high priority to the client (e.g. aesthetically pleasing, adequate space, etc.). Therefore, the implementation

Table 5.6. Design attributes and target values for the family house project

Notation	Design attribute	Unit of measurement	Target value
D1	Energy efficiency	$KgCO_2/m^2$ per annum (for new homes)	36
D2	Impact sound transmission	Decibels (dB)	Not more than 40
D3	Airborne sound transmission	Decibels (dB)	Not more than 30
D4	Flexibility of spaces	Number of party walls	Minimum
D5	Gross floor area	Square metres (m^2)	350
D6	Quality of finish to external envelope	Number of unplanned repairs per annum	Not more than 3
D7	Number of access points to house	Number	Not more than 4
D8	Fresh air supply (outdoor supply of air)	Litres/second per person (l/s)	Minimum of 4·72
D9	Level of internal finish	Average cleaning time per person per day	2 hours
		Number of unplanned repairs per annum	Not more than 4

of high-priority design attributes, offers the possibility of greater client satisfaction. The design attributes, their relative weight, and the target value for each design attribute (constraints), constitute the solution-neutral specifications. Figure 5.4 shows a possible outcome for the family house project.

Figure 5.4. A typical house that could be the outcome of the family house project

5.3.2. University building project

This second example on the use of the CRPM utilises the actual requirements for a building project, which involved the refurbishment, alteration and extension of an existing building at a UK university. However, because the alterations and extensions to the existing building were very extensive, it could be considered as a new build — 75% of the old building was demolished and the portion that was retained made up less than 10% of the new facility. Although the CRPM was not used in the planning of this facility, the requirements for the facility are being used to demonstrate how they could have been processed. The weightings assigned are based on interviews with project participants, the authors' familiarity with the project and a review of some of the project documents.

The project was initiated by one of the academic schools in the university (the School of Science and Technology (SST)). The building that housed most of its technology laboratories, and that was constructed in the 1960s, had outlived its usefulness and needed to be refurbished. This need was seen as an opportunity, by the school administration, to address other needs, which included:

- the need for a focal point for the school, bringing together an otherwise fragmented SST zone within the university
- the need to have a building that reflected the image of the school

- the need to form a partnership with local industry through the creation of an Innovation Resource Centre.

Therefore, the new facility was required to provide accommodation for:

- the SST (technology and computer laboratories, academic offices and seminar space)
- university partnership companies (offices, reception and flexible laboratory space for local enterprises)
- a virtual reality centre
- the university at large (lecture theatre and seminar rooms).

The requirements for the facility are listed in Table 5.7, which consists of two columns. The first column lists the initial requirements developed within SST and the second column is the list developed with other university authorities (e.g. representatives of the Estate Department, etc.).

5.3.2.1 *Define client requirements*

As was mentioned earlier in the chapter (Section 5.2.1), the 'define client requirements' stage of the CRPM is used to document information in a consistent manner, although the type of information can be varied. In this particular case, the stated requirements (Table 5.7) can be restated to capture the functions and attributes of the facility (Table 5.8). It can be observed from the information requirements for the CRPM in Chapter 4 (Figure 4.6) that the rationale for facility functions and attributes should be captured. Information on the meaning of attributes should also be captured. In Table 5.8, for example, the rationale for the function 'create a positive impression to visitors' is that 'the image of SST and the university needs to be enhanced by the quality of its buildings'. Similarly, the additional information against each attribute provides an explanation on what that attribute means. Thus, 'welcoming to visitors' means that the atmosphere (light, temperature, smell, etc.) should make someone feel welcome. 'Cost-effective to run' refers to the level of maintenance costs in relation to the university average and energy consumption in relation to expected limits for similar buildings. The functions and attributes allow clients to relate to the business need behind the facility being commissioned. The information on rationale, and the meaning of attributes, provides justification and facilitates clarity in stating requirements in the language the client understands (his or her 'voice').

Table 5.7. Details of outline and secondary briefs for the university building project

Outline brief (developed within the SST)	Secondary brief (developed with the university)
Prestigious building particularly with respect to external appearance	Single point of access to the building and to each lab space is required to promote security through staff monitoring — this will be reinforced by controlled access systems e.g. SWIPE cards or key button pads
A building which, internally, provides an open/welcoming environment	
A building that establishes security as a priority: limited points of entry/exit; switch card operation (if affordable); main entrance reception for visitors	A preference was expressed for entry to the building from the south where car parking is to be provided. This could be integrated into a courtyard space with soft landscaping
A building to be networked throughout and to include a mix of: heavy engineering laboratories; computer labs; support for small-to-medium enterprises (SMEs); offices; teaching space as available	North elevation should address the streetscape of a major road, as it is a major frontage for the university
Engineering laboratories to be located in zones with emphasis on open planning, flexible space, moveable equipment wherever possible; lightweight partitioning as appropriate	The new facility will become the front door to the school (SST) and should present an appropriate image
SME provision to be various and as available	The existing school is spread over a number of buildings and lacks any focal point or communal space — the opportunities exist in this project to address this
Office accommodation based normally on two persons per room; senior staff in individual rooms	

5.3.2.2 Requirements analysis

The structuring of client requirements (into primary, secondary and tertiary requirements), the prioritisation of interest groups and the prioritisation of tertiary requirements, were all carried out using the procedure described in the previous example of the family house project. The results of these exercises are presented in Tables 5.9 and 5.10, and in Figure 5.5. As was mentioned earlier, the structuring process is aimed at

Table 5.8. Restated requirements for the facility (university building project)

Facility	Rationale
Functions	
Provide adequate space for various activities	The facility is to be used for various purposes
Enhance the image of the university	The university needs to improve its profile through the magnificence of its buildings
Provide security to its users	The building will be used by a wide range of people; adequate security is therefore required
Minimise energy emissions to the environment	This is in keeping with the university's energy policy
Create a positive impression to visitors	The image of SST and the university needs to be enhanced by the quality of its buildings
Provide a focal point for all SST activities	SST activities are fragmented across the university and this does not help with its image
Enhance productivity of staff and students	Users should be made comfortable so that they can do their work better
Attributes	
Welcoming to visitors (i.e. the atmosphere — light, temperature, smell, etc. — should make someone feel welcome)	Many external visitors are expected to use the facility
Cost-effective to run (i.e. maintenance expenditure below university average per m² and energy consumption within expected limits for similar facilities)	To minimise estate expenditure and supplement the budgets of other activities within the university
Aesthetically pleasing (i.e. external envelope should be very attractive to the normal viewer)	The physical outlook of the university needs enhancement

Table 5.8. continued

Facility	Rationale
Comfortable (with respect to lights, heating, ventilation, space provision to users, etc.)	The university is an investor in people and therefore seeks the welfare of its staff, students and visitors
Flexible (i.e. it is easy to redefine the use of spaces depending on the changing needs of the university)	The university has to respond to changes in technology and student enrolment on courses
Accessible to SST industrial partners (i.e. industrial partners should be able to use the facility when necessary)	The basis of funding was the partnership with local businesses

identifying and mapping strategic (high-level) and tactical requirements. The information on the rationale for functions and attributes can inform this process. For example, there are several phrases that emphasise the need for the university to present a good image through its buildings. Thus, it can be inferred that a strategic (primary) requirement is for the university to have 'an impressive innovation resource centre' (Figure 5.5).

Table 5.9. Absolute and relative weights for interest groups

Notation	Name of group	Raw score (AW_r)	Relative weight (RW_r)
A	SST management	14	10·00
B	SST academic staff	6	4·28
C	University Estate Department	10	7·14
D	Corporate and Commercial Department	8	5·71
E	Virtual Reality Centre staff	8	5·71
F	Students (SST and other)	6	4·28
G	SST technicians	9	6·43
H	University management	13	9·28

Table 5.10. *Prioritisation of tertiary requirements*

Interest group	Rel. wt	Adequate space for various functions	Adequate security	Easy access by all users	Open and pleasant internal environment	Low maintenance costs	Low operating costs	Blends with streetscape	Blends with other university buildings	Aesthetically pleasing
SST management	3·94	7	8	5	7	9	6	8	6	9
SST academic staff	1·69	8	6	4	8	7	4	5	6	7
University Estate Department	2·81	5	9	7	4	8	9	7	7	9
Corporate and Commercial Department	2·25	9	5	5	7	5	5	5	5	7
Virtual Reality Centre	2·25	9	8	4	8	6	5	5	5	6
Students	1·69	5	4	7	6	5	4	5	3	6
SST technicians	2·53	9	5	6	7	8	5	5	4	7
University management	3·66	7	7	3	4	9	9	8	7	9
Absolute weight		152	141	104	129	156	131	132	117	163
Relative weight of requirements		9·73	8·68	6·41	7·9	9·6	8·02	8·15	7·16	10

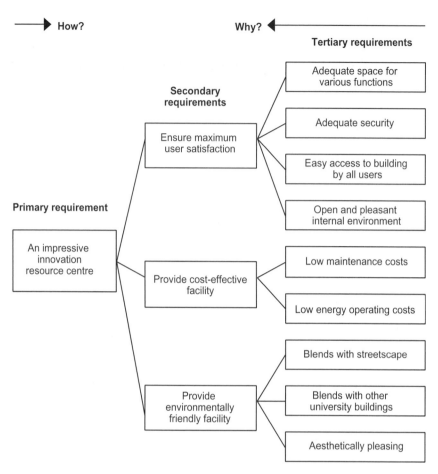

Figure 5.5. Primary, secondary and tertiary requirements for the university building project

It is also worth noting how the relative importance of interest groups influences the final relative weights of each tertiary requirement. In prioritising interest groups, the pair-wise ratings need to reflect the influence of an interest group in the acquisition of the facility and the effects the facility will have on them. For example, 'SST management' have the highest score because of their important role in initiating the project and raising funds to finance it.

5.3.2.3 Requirements translation

The generation of design attributes for this facility, determination of target values, mapping of tertiary requirements to design attributes, and the determination of the absolute and relative weights of design attributes, are carried out in accordance with the procedures used in the previous example. However, it should be noted that the design attributes and target values for this example (Table 5.11) are slightly different, and

Table 5.11. Design attributes for the university building project

Notation	Design attribute	Unit of measurement	Target value
D1	Gross floor area	Square metres (m²)	6000
D2	Number of access points	Number	3
D3	Quality of finish to interior	Number of unplanned repairs per annum	Less than 5
D4	Supply of fresh air for users	Litres/second per person (l/s)	10
D5	Dry resultant temp.	Degrees Celsius (°C)	20
D6	Air velocity	Metres per second (m/s)	0·1
D7	Relative humidity	Per cent	60
D8	Reverberation time within spaces	Seconds	0·5
D9	Energy efficiency	Calculated credits	12
D10	Strong architectural expression	Subjective measurement	Depends on client
D11	Quality of finish to external envelope	Number of unplanned repairs per annum	Less than 3
D12	Control and operation of lighting and heating, ventilation and air-conditioning (HVAC)	Extent to which user can alter controls	70% control by user
D13	Segregation of spaces	Number of associated sections	Not more than 6

Table 5.12. Matrix for translating tertiary requirements for the university building project (a blank signifies no relationship)

Tertiary requirements	Rel. wt	Gross floor area	No. of access points	Quality of finish to interior	Supply of fresh air for users	Dry resultant temperature	Air velocity	Rel. humidity	Reverberation time within spaces	Energy efficiency	Strong architectural expression to external envelope	Quality Control/ finish of lighting and HVAC	Segregation of operation of spaces
Adequate space for various functions	9·37	9	1	3	9	1	3	3	3	3	3	1	9
Adequate security	8·68	3	9						1			3	9
Easy access to all users	6·41	3	9		1						3	1	9
Open and pleasant internal environment	7·9	9	1	9	9	9	9	9	9	9	3	9	9
Low maintenance costs	9·6	9		3					1	1	9	9	3
Low operating costs	8·02	3	3	9	9	9	9	9	1	9	3	9	3

	Importance													
Blends with streetscape	8·15									9	9		
Blends with other university buildings	7·16	1								9	9		
Aesthetically pleasing	10	3	3							9	9		1
Absolute weight (design attributes)		311	214	230	234	153	171	171	126	181	409	419	171	354
Relative weight (design attributes)		7·4	5·1	5·5	5·6	3·6	4·1	4·1	3	4·3	9·8	10	4·1	8·5

that there are cases where a quantitative measurement cannot be made (e.g. subjective measurement for 'strong architectural expression'). The relationship matrix (Table 5.12) shows that the 'quality of finish to the exterior' is the design attribute with the highest relative weight. This reflects the importance the interest groups with the highest relative weight place on aesthetics (the building as a 'front door' for the school). Figure 5.6 shows the completed building.

5.3.3 Road bypass project

An example on the use of the CRPM to establish client requirements on civil engineering projects is now considered. The Newbury Bypass project, which was one of the most controversial road-building projects in the UK, is used in this illustration (Bypass, 2000).

5.3.3.1 Brief background to the project

The aim of the Newbury Bypass project was to alleviate the flow of traffic on the A34 (the Midlands to Southampton trunk road) through the town of Newbury. Prior to this, the A34, which was built as a dual carriageway in the 1960s, extended for two miles through built-up areas of Newbury and, while roundabouts and flyovers had been built to ease congestion, it was frequently the scene of major traffic jams, particularly at the junction with another major road (the A4) (ICE, 1997; Bypass, 2000). The various reasons for traffic congestion included the growth of the town since the

Figure 5.6. Completed university building

road was built, the increase in car ownership in the area and the meeting of east–west and north–south traffic streams (ICE, 1997; Bypass, 2000). While much has been written about this very controversial project, the focus here is to illustrate the use of the CRPM to establish the requirements of the client. In this exercise, the road is the 'facility' that was supposed to meet the business need (i.e. traffic congestion) of the 'client' and the analysis will start, as specified by the CRPM, after the 'decision to build' had been taken (i.e. the decision to build a bypass around the town).

5.3.3.2   Define client requirements

A key to the 'define client requirements' activity for a project like this is the identification of the components of the client (as defined in Chapter 1) and those who will influence, and be affected by, the acquisition, operation and disposal of the facility. These interest groups include the Highways Agency, other government departments, the local government authority, local residents, politicians (both local and national), motorists, environmental and other pressure groups (e.g. the roads lobby, Friends of the Earth, etc.), and relevant statutory bodies. Some of the reasons for the project, as recorded in published documents (ICE, 1997; Bypass, 2000), are used here to define the functions and attributes of the facility, which are summarised in Table 5.13.

Other information that should be captured at this stage includes acquisition information (allowable budget, expected duration, appointed representatives of the client, etc.), operation information (whether a toll system is preferred, effective speed management, etc.), and disposal information (e.g. expected lifespan, future plans, etc.).

5.3.3.3   Requirements analysis

This involves the structuring of requirements into primary, secondary and tertiary requirements (Figure 5.7), the prioritisation of interest groups and the prioritisation of tertiary requirements, using the techniques employed in previous examples.

An examination of the list of functions and attributes for the road in Table 5.13 reveals that there is repeated reference to the safety and quality of life for local residents. This suggests that a strategic need (primary requirement) for the project is the improvement of the quality of life for local residents. Another strategic need could be the need to implement government plans for road building (Figure 5.7). It must be noted that although it is assumed in this example that the decision to build a bypass

Table 5.13. Functions and attributes of the bypass road project

Road project	Rationale
Functions	
Provide a single direct route that stretches the length of the country	There is a need for the traffic from the European continent to be able to move easily between Southampton (a sea port) and Birmingham (the second largest city in England)
Reduce the amount of traffic passing through the centre of Newbury	Traffic through the town centre causes congestion and traffic jams, and poses a risk to local residents. The bypass will divert non-local traffic away from the town
Reduce journey times	The reduction of journey times through less congestion will facilitate the smooth operation of business activities. Extra costs caused by congestion can ultimately lead to bankruptcy
Reduce pollution	This is necessary to increase the quality of life of local residents
Minimise the disruption to local traffic and pedestrian movement	Since the A34 goes through the town, out-of-town traffic causes congestion and disruption to local traffic
Improve the quality of life of the citizens in the town	Increased traffic causes pollution through noise and the discharge of exhaust fumes. The vibration from heavy traffic also causes damage to structures
Attributes	
Environmentally sustainable (i.e. environmental issues and concerns are duly taken into consideration)	Protection of the natural and built environment is at the heart of government policy
Cost-effective to construct (i.e. the most economical solution should be pursued)	The government seeks to be prudent in its use of public funds

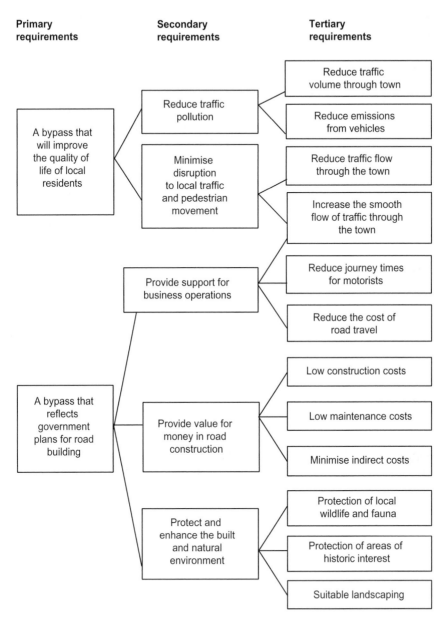

Figure 5.7. Primary, secondary and tertiary requirements for bypass project

had already been taken, the structuring process can be used to test the validity of the proposed solution (i.e. the road bypass) to improve the quality of life of local residents. For example, a bypass road around the town will 'reduce traffic volume through the town' if the main cause of traffic congestion is due to non-local traffic. However, if congestion is due to increased car ownership in the town (as was intimated by some of the environmental groups opposed to the bypass — Bypass, 2000), then an alternative solution should be considered.

With regard to the prioritisation of interest groups and tertiary requirements, the relative importance of each interest group should be assessed with respect to their influence on the acquisition, use and operation of the facility, and on the effect of the road on them. Some reports on the project alleged that the concerns of environmental pressure groups were not adequately incorporated, although the protests from such groups considerably affected the construction (acquisition) of the road by significantly increasing the cost of security (Bypass, 2000). On the other hand, the extensive consultation process and public enquiries for this project (and similar schemes) (ICE, 1997) provides a good opportunity to assess the relative weightings that different interest groups place on various requirements.

5.3.3.4 Requirements translation

The procedure for translating (mapping) requirements to design attributes is the same as in the previous examples. However, since this is a different project type, the design attributes will be different. Table 5.14 provides a list of design attributes and suggested target values, which were compiled from a Highways Agency document on route management strategies (Highways Agency, 2000). In generating this list, attention was paid to the requirements for the project to ensure that the technical specifications (design attributes) selected will satisfy the tertiary requirements. For example, the following tertiary requirements (Figure 5.7), 'reduce traffic volume through town', 'reduce journey times for motorists', 'reduce the cost of travel', etc., could be satisfied, to varying degrees, by the design attribute 'minimum traffic congestion', which deals with the congestion delays. Similarly, 'protection of local wildlife and fauna' and 'suitable landscaping' could be satisfied by the design attributes 'adequate biodiversity action plan' and 'appropriate land management plans'.

The design attributes are technical performance (solution-neutral) specifications that have implications for design. For example, to satisfy the 'minimum traffic congestion' target, consideration will have to be

Table 5.14. *Sample design attributes for the bypass road project*

Notation	Design attribute	Unit of measurement	Target value
D1	Minimum traffic congestion	Peak average time delay per vehicle km	Less than 10 seconds
D2	Low accident rates	Personal injury accidents (PIA) per 100 vehicle km	Not more than 15
D3	Minimum noise exposure	Noise severity index expressed as the number of properties per km where people are expected — level above 68 dBA	Less than 10
D4	Adequate biodiversity action plan	Per cent of road section for which a plan exists	Greater than 75%
D5	Appropriate land management plans	Per cent of road section for which a plan exists	Greater than 75%
D6	Minimum hindrance to non-motorised road users (e.g. number of at grade pedestrian crossings)	A score reflecting the need of users and quality of facilities on a scale of 5 (highest) to 1 (lowest hindrance to non-motorised road users)	1
D7	Adequate road facilities (e.g. emergency telephones, lay-bys)	Availability of facilities score on a scale of 5 (least facilities) to 1 (most facilities)	1
D8	Road capacity (i.e. traffic volume on new bypass)	Proportion of traffic volumes passing through town	At least 50%
D9	Flexibility to handle future growth	Projected traffic (PT) volumes over the design life	Road should handle at least 90% of PT

Figure 5.8. A section of the Newbury bypass during construction (courtesy of New Civil Engineer Magazine*)*

given to project traffic volumes, physical properties of the road (e.g. number of carriageways), and the traffic management scheme for the road (e.g. speed limits). Similarly, the 'minimum noise exposure' design attribute will affect the design of road surfacing in the vicinity of properties, location of embankments and cuttings, etc. Thus, by systematically mapping tertiary requirements (which relate to strategic business needs) to design attributes, proposed designs can easily be checked to see if they incorporate the 'voice of the client'. Figure 5.8 shows a section of the Newbury Bypass during construction.

5.4   General observations on the use of the CRPM

The aforementioned examples have sought to illustrate how the CRPM can be used to capture clients' requirements on construction projects. These have demonstrated the systematic way in which clients' business needs are analysed and mapped on to tactical and technical specifications that are solution-neutral. A few observations on the wider application of the model and potential challenges that might arise from its use are now discussed.

5.4.1 Wider application of the CRPM

Although the CRPM is designed to be used *after* the decision to build has been made, it is possible to use it earlier or later on in the overall construction process. In the 'conceive project stage' (Figure 5.1) it can be used to analyse the client's statement of need to decide whether or not a built solution is the most appropriate answer to his or her problem. The underlying principle of moving from 'strategic to tactical' can be used to explore the various solutions to the client's strategic need. The structuring of requirements for the bypass road project in Section 5.3.3.3 above showed that the decomposition of the strategic (primary) need to 'improve the quality of life of local residents' might have led to a different solution. However, even if the CRPM is not used much earlier in the process, the example of the road project shows that it can still be used to question earlier decisions.

With regard to later stages of the construction process (e.g. the design and construction stage in Figure 5.1), the techniques used in the CRPM can be used to 'translate' design attributes to design concepts, and to move design concepts to components of the facility, etc. This follows the principle of systematic deployment of 'quality' features throughout the product development process, which is characteristic of the QFD methodology (see Chapter 3).

5.4.2 The CRPM and iteration

The systematic way in which the CRPM is used to establish client requirements might suggest a linear process that does not support iteration. However, this is not the case, as there can be iteration both within each stage and over the entire process. The structuring of requirements within the 'analyse client requirements' stage of the model is one example of iteration within a stage. The use of the value tree analysis technique ensures that the decomposition of strategic client requirements to tactical (tertiary) requirements is iterative.

Iteration is also possible between different stages. In the example of the bypass road project, it was observed that questions about the client's decision to construct a road as a solution to the problems of congestion are challenged during the 'analyse client requirements' stage. This can lead to a re-examination of whether the road is the right solution to the strategic need of residents — improved quality of life, etc.

Thus, instead of restricting iteration, the CRPM enhances it by providing a structured and systematic means for tracing requirements as they are captured and processed. This can even extend to the design stage, where, for example, the proposed solution to meet target values for comfort can force a rethink of the intended operation and management strategy specified by the client in the requirements processing stage.

5.4.3   *The use of sketches/visualisations in the CRPM*

The CRPM is designed to allow the 'processing' of client requirements without the use of sketches, as is the case in current briefing practice (see Chapter 2). However, it is acknowledged that the use of sketches and visual aids might be unavoidable. For example, in the refurbishment of an existing facility, it is obvious that drawings of the existing building will be used. This possibility, although not specified in the illustrative examples discussed earlier in the chapter, has been allowed for in the 'translate client requirements' stage of the CRPM, where the determination of target values specifies the use of 'other information'. This can include the use of photographs and other visual representations of, say, existing and/or similar facilities. However, it must be stressed that with the CRPM, sketches and visual tools do not provide the primary means for 'processing' and establishing the clients' requirements.

5.4.4   *Some challenges in utilising the CRPM*

Some of the challenges that might be encountered by an RPT include the identification of interest groups, determination of their relative importance, and the elicitation of their weightings on the requirements for a project. The identification of interest groups should be based on interviews with the representative(s) of the client, and the experience of the RPT on similar projects. Where interest groups are located within one organisation (e.g. the university building project), their views can be elicited through various ways, such as questionnaire surveys, focus group discussions, workshops and meetings with representatives of such groups. However, the determination of their relative importance can be tricky because a particular group might not appreciate the fact that they have been given a relatively low rating, although that may be perfectly justifiable in a given circumstance. A way around this is to ask each group to rate (using criteria weighting) the importance of other groups with respect to the project under consideration, and aggregating the scores.

However, when interest groups are external to the organisation that is commissioning a project (e.g. in the case of a road project), eliciting the views of interest groups can be even more difficult. It is advisable, in these cases, to have consultations very early on in the process, even before planning approval is sought for a project.

It should be recognised that the use of the CRPM is not a 'one-day affair', as some weightings and decisions will have to be investigated. For example, consultations with interest groups to determine their preferences, determining target values, etc. It should also be noted that solution-neutral design specifications, the final output of the CRPM, are, in themselves, not sufficient for design — these have to be combined with site conditions and other factors to provide a proper context for design Therefore, it is suggested that the establishment of client requirements should be carried out in parallel with other activities, such as site studies, and the overall context for design (client requirements and possible 'constraints') are defined.

5.4.5   Limitations of the CRPM

An underlying assumption of the CRPM is that the person/organisation commissioning a project will incorporate the views of interest groups. So, if there is an unwillingness to incorporate these views, the model will be limited in its application, although requirements can still be prioritised using criteria weighting without any reference to interest groups.

The implementation of the model is also time consuming and, within the current culture in the construction industry where insufficient time is spent in defining client requirements, this approach might not be welcome by some sectors of the industry. Furthermore, if the model is implemented by a design team, they may be constrained by design targets, and may consider the approach represented by the model to be unnecessary. Indeed, the model was designed to be implemented by a separate RPT. Undoubtedly, this will increase the client's costs but the overall benefits far outweigh these costs.

The limitation of too much time spent on processing client requirements can be minimised by computerisation of the model. This will further enhance the usefulness of the model and provide a basis for its integration with other activities in the construction process, which are already computer-based. The next chapter describes a prototype software that was developed to address this limitation.

Chapter 6

ClientPro: software version of the client requirements processing model

6.1 Overview of Chapter 6

This chapter describes the development and utilisation of a prototype software called ClientPro for the establishment of client requirements on construction projects. ClientPro is based on the client requirements processing model (CRPM) and was developed to enhance the use of the model. One of the examples in the previous chapter is used to illustrate the practical use of the prototype. The results of an evaluation of ClientPro by construction industry practitioners are also presented.

6.2 Objectives of ClientPro

The objective of ClientPro is to facilitate the establishment of client requirements (as prescribed in the CRPM) within a computer environment. This is intended to enhance the management of client requirements processing (i.e. the documentation, generation, correlation and traceability of client requirements) and the future integration of client requirements processing with other computer-based design and construction activities. Thus, ClientPro was designed to:

- allow the entry, storage, viewing and editing of information required for processing client requirements at any stage in the processing activity
- facilitate the calculation of absolute and relative weights for client interest groups, tertiary requirements and design attributes

- allow the processing of requirements for different 'client' and 'project types'
- facilitate the traceability of requirements as they are developed and processed, and the reuse of previously stored information
- facilitate the generation of design attributes and the determination of their target values, using previously defined information and other sources of information
- be easy to use with adequate instructions on how to carry out the processing of client requirements
- facilitate the generation and printing of reports on various aspects and outputs of the model
- allow for future extension of the system and integration with other computer-based downstream design and construction activities.

6.3 Development of ClientPro

To ensure that the desired features and objectives of ClientPro are satisfied, the system architecture for the prototype, which is illustrated in Figure 6.1, was developed. Three modules provide the means for requirements definition, analysis and translation. These modules facilitate the storage and retrieval of information from the data storage facility. The user interface interacts with all three modules, which are interconnected. The arrows linking the modules indicate that entry, storage, viewing and editing of information can be done at any stage in the processing activity.

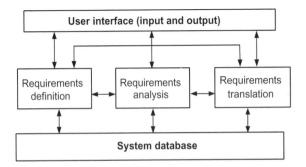

Figure 6.1. System architecture for ClientPro

6.3.1   Selection of implementation environment

The implementation environment for prototypes and general system development is usually based on a number of options, which, according to Britton and Doake (1996), include:

- programming in a procedural, third-generation language (3GL) (e.g. FORTRAN), where the programmer has to describe in detail how every task is to be carried out
- programming in a problem-oriented fourth-generation language (4GL) (e.g. C, C++), where the programmer merely has to define what must be done
- using a general-purpose integrated package that incorporates facilities such as word processing, spreadsheets, database and report generators
- use and customisation of specific application (commercial) packages.

In the development of ClientPro, a general-purpose database package (Microsoft Access) was chosen for the implementation of the CRPM. This was due to a number of factors, which included the vital role database systems play in the management of requirements (see Chapter 3) and the need to develop quickly the prototype at minimal expense. The choice of Microsoft (MS) Access was also based on the fact that its capacity is sufficient to allow for future extension. It also contains querying and connective capabilities that facilitate data navigation and the minimisation of redundant data storage. Furthermore, MS Access has been used in similar research dealing with the capture and management of requirements (Tseng and Jiao, 1998; Morris *et al.*, 1998).

It is acknowledged that relational database systems may have limitations, when compared to object-oriented database management systems (OODBMSs), in the handling of complex data types and in their overall management (Taschek, 1997). However, the availability of MS Access in a format that facilitates the development of database applications, as opposed to the relatively new OODBMS technology, made it more appropriate in the development of ClientPro.

6.3.2   Development of ClientPro within Microsoft Access

The development of ClientPro followed the general procedure for developing MS Access applications. An MS Access application is a coordinated set of database objects — tables, forms, macros, queries, reports and modules — that enable the user to maintain the data contained in a database (McLaren, 1996). The development of an MS Access application involves the evaluation of the information needs of the system, with particular reference to the flow of data and information (see information model for the CRPM in Chapter 4), and the design of the database objects that will solve the information problems.

The development of tables, queries, forms, reports and macros for ClientPro was carried out using the facilities provided within MS Access. The design of tables was based on the information model (see Figures 4.4 to 4.7), which also provided the basis for specifying the relationships between tables. Each table represented an entity, corresponding to the defined entities in Table 6.1 (a modified version of Table 4.2). The entity attributes constituted the 'fields' (or columns) of respective tables. Figure 6.2 shows the relationships between some tables in ClientPro. The symbols '1' and '∞' at both ends of a line indicate a 'one-to-many' relationship between the two tables. For example, there is a one-to-many relationship between 'primary requirements' and 'secondary requirements'. This means that for each primary requirement, there can be one or more secondary requirements. The relationship between 'proposed facility use' (activities performed) and 'user information' is indicated as 'one-to-many' because one activity can be performed by many different users. It is, however, possible for one user to perform many activities in a facility (i.e. a many-to-many relationship).

Queries were used in the development of features that facilitated the analysis of requirements, the prioritisation of client interest groups, tertiary client requirements and design attributes. They also allowed the creation of matrices for pair-wise comparisons to determine the relative importance of interest groups and in the translation of TCRs into design attributes. Command buttons, which were mostly based on macros, together with customised menu items, were used in the development of the user interface. Table 6.2 provides a summary of how the desired features of ClientPro (see Section 6.2 above) were implemented in the development process.

6.4   Utilisation of ClientPro

Running ClientPro requires the installation of MS Access. When the file containing ClientPro is opened, a welcome screen is displayed (Figure 6.3). This leads to a 'control' form with buttons that open all the forms for

Table 6.1. Attributes for defined entities in the CRPM

Entity group	Entity	Attributes
Client/project characteristics	Client details	Name, address, business type, contact person's name and address, number of employees, average annual turnover, policy on occupancy/space use
	Interest groups	Name, type, relationship with client, influence in acquisition and use of facility, effect of facility acquisition, operation and use on group
	Project details	Project name, location, type, facility type, facility objectives
Client business need	Use information	Activity type, time of day performed, time of year performed, peak use times, required equipment and furniture
	User information	User name, user type, user size, relationship with client, activity performed
	Facility functions	Function verb, function noun, function qualifier, function rationale (i.e. why a specific function is required)
	Facility attributes	Attribute name, attribute meaning, attribute rationale, function associated with attribute
Facility process	Acquisition information	Available budget, rationale for budget, level of client involvement (risk), rationale for level of client involvement, client representatives, expected date of completion, rationale for completion date
	Operation information	Costs in use (CIU), meaning and rationale for CIU, operation management strategy (OMS), rationale for OMS, level of operation management technology (OMT), rationale for OMT
	Disposal information	Expected lifespan, rationale for expected lifespan, etc.
Other sources of information	International standards	Standards for the expression of user requirements, standards for air capacity for occupants in specified building types, etc.
	Benchmark/ other info.	Operation/maintenance information for existing/similar facilities, etc.

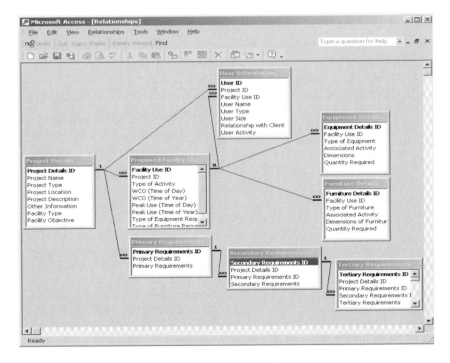

Figure 6.2. Relationships between some tables in ClientPro

viewing, editing and processing client requirements. Forms and reports can also be accessed from menus. Figure 6.4 is a schematic diagram showing the operation and flow of forms in ClientPro. The use of ClientPro in establishing client requirements will be illustrated using the requirements for the university building project described in Chapter 5.

6.4.1   Defining client requirements

This involves the input of information on:

- the project
- the client
- interest groups represented by the client
- proposed use and users
- the functions and attributes of the facility
- information on the acquisition, operation and disposal of the facility.

Table 6.2. Summary of how required features for ClientPro were implemented

Required feature	How it was satisfied in ClientPro
Allow the entry, storage, viewing and editing of information at any stage in the processing activity	Designed forms allowed the display and editing of stored data
	The customised menu included on every form facilitated the display/editing of information at any stage of the requirements process
	The development of more than one form for a given table, in some cases, also facilitated the display and editing of information at appropriate stages in the processing activity
Facilitate the calculation of absolute and relative weights for client interest groups, tertiary requirements and design attributes	The use of queries and the embedded MS Excel spreadsheet through the 'pivot tables', allowed the entry of formulae for the calculation of absolute and relative weights; therefore, calculations are performed automatically
Allow the processing of requirements for different client and project types	Although the predefined list of options in drop-down combination boxes were more biased to building projects, they are not restrictive, as the user can enter his or her preferences. Therefore, it should be possible to use ClientPro for a wide range of client and project types
Facilitate the traceability of requirements as they are developed and processed, and the reuse of previously stored information	This was facilitated by the development of more than one form per table, in some cases
	The insertion of sub-forms also facilitated the reuse of stored information at a later stage in the processing activity
Facilitate the generation of design attributes and the determination of target values	The drop-down list of suggested design attributes facilitated the generation of design attributes, as it prompts the user on what constitutes a design attribute
	The entry and storage of target values could also be done in ClientPro, however, to be more useful, an automated process for determining target values is needed

Table 6.2. continued

Required feature	How it was satisfied in ClientPro
Easy to use with adequate instructions on how to carry out the processing activity	Although the 'Help' menu was not implemented in ClientPro, every effort was made to ensure that forms were clear and unambiguous
	Guidance was also provided on every control by written instructions in the 'status bar text' property of those controls. This ensures that when a button or text box receives the focus, a text appears on the status bar of the form to explain what action is required
Facilitate the generation and printing of reports on various information	Several reports, which summarised and/or combined certain kinds of information, were designed
	Appropriate macros and buttons were also designed to open these reports
Allow for future extension and integration with other computer-based construction activities	The ease with which it is possible to add other tables to ClientPro should facilitate its extension
	As an application in the MS Office group, MS Access can be successfully linked with other packages, such as MS Excel, other database systems, and AutoCAD

Various forms are used to input, edit and view data relating to the project. All these forms can be accessed by clicking on the appropriate buttons on the control form (Figure 6.5) or by selecting one of the options on the 'Processing/Definition' menu item.

6.4.1.1 Example on inputting information

As an example of the kind of forms used, Figure 6.6 shows the forms for entering, viewing and editing data about the functions of the facility. The labels are designed to be self-explanatory and the user is also provided with further information (instructions and explanation) on

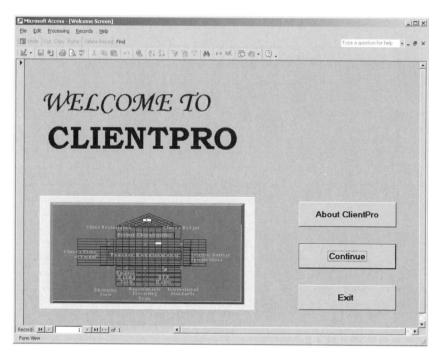

Figure 6.3. Welcome screen in ClientPro

the status bar at the bottom of the form. At the top of the form, there are spaces for 'project ID' and 'functions ID'. The identification number (in this case '1') for the project under consideration has to be entered in the space for 'project ID'. The identification number for the facility functions are generated automatically when a new entry is to be made. However, because of the relationship between the project and the functions, the project ID always has to be specified, otherwise a new entry for facility functions will not be saved (this also applies to all other forms in ClientPro). Facility functions are defined using a 'verb', 'noun' and a 'function qualifier'. The user selects from drop-down combination lists, or enters the verbs, nouns and 'qualifiers' that best describe a function of the proposed facility. There is also provision for the user to indicate why a specific function is necessary (function rationale) for satisfying the business need of the client. Entry for the next function is facilitated by clicking the 'next' button or by using the MS Access data controls at the bottom of the form. Other forms for entering, viewing and editing data provide similar features and user interaction.

124

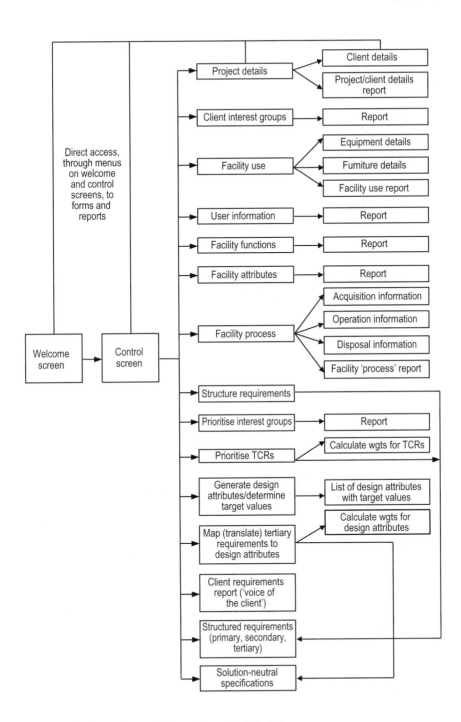

Figure 6.4. Operation and flow of forms in ClientPro

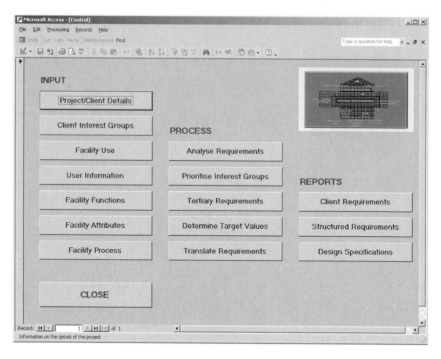

Figure 6.5. Control form showing buttons to all other forms

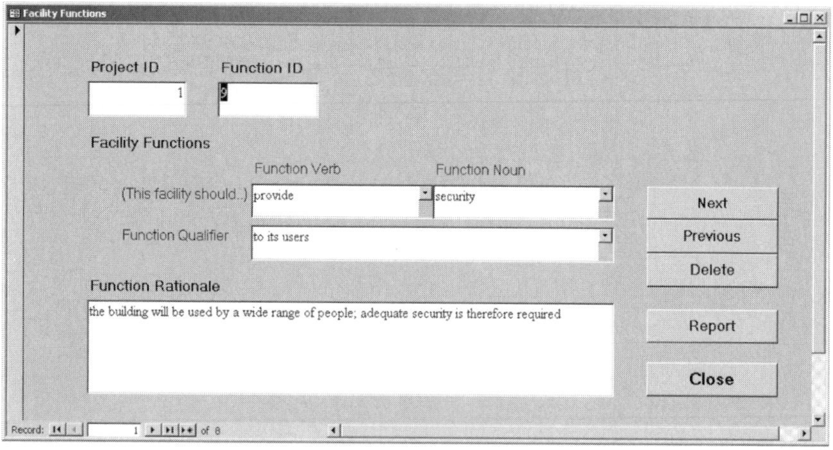

Figure 6.6. Facility functions form

6.4.1.2 Reports on input information

Figures 6.7 and 6.8 show a sample of the reports generated by ClientPro. These are for facility functions and attributes, and facility process (acquisition, operation and disposal information). The facility functions and attributes report combines the individual reports for functions and attributes.

6.4.2 Analysing client requirements

The analysis of client requirements involves the structuring of requirements into primary, secondary and tertiary requirements, the prioritisation of client interest groups and the prioritising of tertiary requirements, using the appropriate forms provided in ClientPro.

6.4.2.1 Structuring of requirements

The form shown in Figure 6.9 is used for the structuring of requirements. The functions and attributes of the facility defined earlier are displayed in

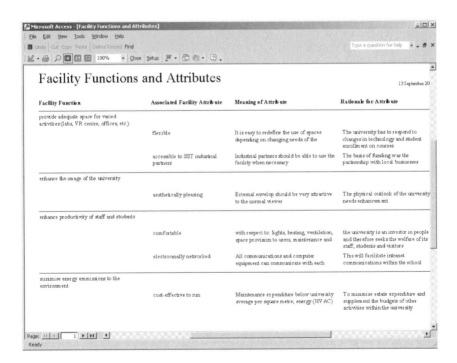

Figure 6.7. Report for facility functions and attributes

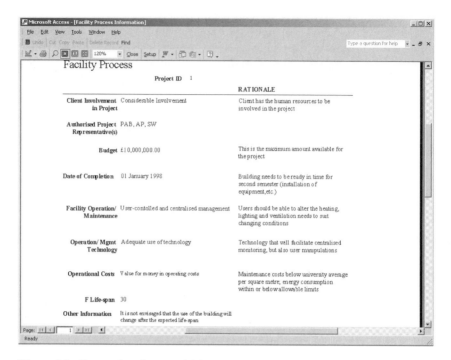

Figure 6.8. Report showing acquisition, operation and disposal information

the top part of the form. Other information that might be useful in structuring the requirements can be accessed from the menu. The form also contains sub-forms for the input, viewing and editing of primary, secondary and tertiary requirements. Each of these forms has three columns. The first two columns provide for identification and cross-reference purposes (e.g. between a primary requirement and its associated secondary requirement), and the third column provides for the entry of primary, secondary or tertiary requirements.

6.4.2.2 Prioritisation of client interest groups

The prioritisation of interest groups is by pair-wise comparisons using the 'client interest groups (CLIG) prioritisation form' illustrated in Figure 6.10. There are two parts to the form — a top section that reproduces the information on each interest group defined earlier for easy reference and a bottom section that provides a matrix for pair-wise comparison of interest groups. The ID and names of interest groups are reproduced in the first two columns of the matrix. Each interest group is

128

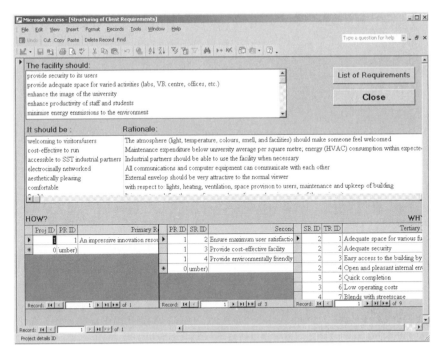

Figure 6.9. Structuring of client requirements

assigned a notation in the form CL1, CL2,...,CL9 (assuming a maximum of nine interest groups) and these are entered in the third column of the matrix.

Following the assignment of notation, each group is then compared to each of the others, and the level of importance of one group over the other is represented either by a 4, 3, 2 or 1 to indicate major importance, medium importance, minor importance and equal importance, respectively. If CL1 is considered to be of major importance over CL2, the number 4 is entered in the CL1 row, under the CL2 column, and 0 is entered in the opposite space on the matrix (i.e. row CL2, column CL1). If the reverse is the case, then the number is entered in the CL2 row, under the CL1 column, and 0 is entered in row CL1, column CL2. When two groups (e.g. CL1 and CL3) are considered to be of equal importance, the number 1 is entered on both sides of the matrix (i.e. on row CL1, column CL3, and row CL3, column CL1). The absolute weight for each interest group is the sum of all the numbers on its corresponding row and this is automatically given in the 'AbsWt' column. The relative weight of each interest group, calculated by rationalising the absolute weights, is given in the 'RelWt' column in the

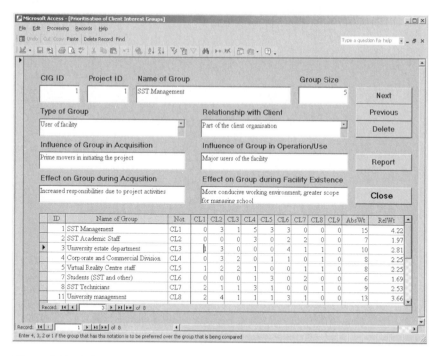

Figure 6.10. Prioritisation of client interest groups

matrix. If required, a report showing the prioritised list of interest groups can be displayed.

6.4.2.3   Prioritisation of tertiary requirements

The prioritisation of tertiary requirements is based on the relative importance of interest groups and the weight each group places on those requirements, and is carried out using the form shown in Figure 6.11.

The top section of the form displays information on previously defined tertiary requirements and their assigned notation. The bottom half of the form is a matrix for entering the weightings assigned by interest groups to each tertiary requirement. The first three columns in the matrix contain the ID numbers, list of interest groups and the relative weights of interest groups determined earlier. The other columns are titled TR01, TR02, up to TR25 (this assumed limit of 25 can be expanded), and correspond to the assigned notation for tertiary requirements.

To prioritise the tertiary requirements, the weighting each interest group places on a tertiary requirement is entered in the appropriate place

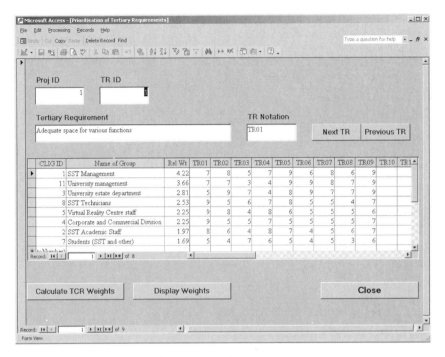

Figure 6.11. Prioritisation of tertiary requirements

in the matrix. A number from 1 to 9 (least important to most important) is used to indicate the level of importance a group places on each of the requirements. After the weightings by interest groups for each tertiary requirement has been entered, the calculated absolute and relative weights are viewed by clicking on a button ('calculate weights') at the bottom of the form. Clicking this button displays a form (Figure 6.12) that contains the list of tertiary requirements (including spaces for absolute and relative weights) and an embedded MS Excel sheet that contains the values for the absolute weights (under the 'total' column) and relative weights, corresponding to the assigned notation for tertiary requirements. The values for absolute and relative weights on the embedded MS Excel sheet are then copied on to the form containing the tertiary requirements.

If the list of tertiary requirements is longer than what can be viewed on the embedded MS Excel sheet, or if information on the interest group/tertiary requirements matrix is being updated, the full MS Excel sheet can be viewed by clicking on the 'edit pivot table' button. If previously entered information is being updated, this can be done by

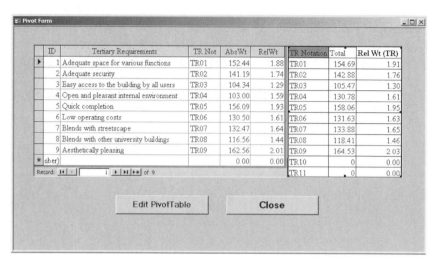

Figure 6.12. Calculated weights for tertiary requirements

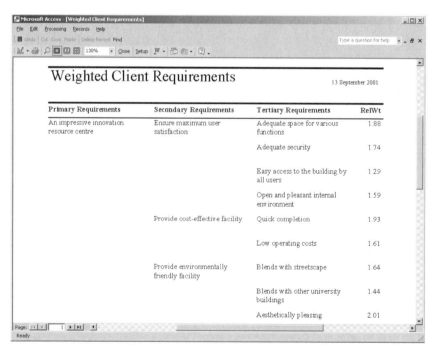

Figure 6.13. Report showing weighted list of tertiary requirements

highlighting the 'total' column, and then selecting 'refresh data' from the 'data' menu item on the MS Excel sheet. This updates the values for the absolute weights (displayed under the 'total' column) and, subsequently, the relative weights for tertiary requirements, which are calculated by normalising the absolute weights. The weighted list of tertiary requirements is shown in Figure 6.13.

6.4.3 Translating client requirements

Requirements translation involves the generation of design attributes, determining target values and associating tertiary requirements with design attributes in a matrix.

6.4.3.1 Design attributes and target values

The 'target values' form (Figure 6.14) provides for both the generation of design attributes and the determination of target values. The top section

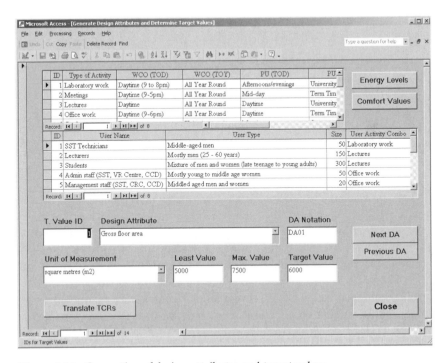

Figure 6.14. Generation of design attributes and target values

of the form contains previously defined information (use and user information, for example) that can be used in determining the target values for design attributes. Other supplementary information, such as energy consumption levels and human comfort values, can be displayed on the form by clicking on the appropriate buttons provided.

Design attributes for the facility are generated by selecting from the drop-down list or by entering a particular attribute in the space provided. A notation in the form, DA01, DA02, etc., is assigned to each attribute, whose target value is determined using the information provided in the top part of the form. The unit of measurement for some target values, which may not be very specific, is indicated as 'subjective measurement'. The target values for other attributes could be stated in the original set of requirements provided by the client. For example, 'gross floor area' for the facility used in this demonstration was specified by the client in the documentation for the project. Where available, targets can be based on past records of the client that are based on similar facilities. One of the target values in this example, 'quality of finish to interior', was defined in terms of the number of unplanned repairs to the interior of the building. In this case, the target value can be set at, or below, the average number of unplanned repairs for other buildings that the client operates.

6.4.3.2 *Translating tertiary requirements into design attributes*

The mapping of tertiary requirements to design attributes is carried out using the form shown in Figure 6.15. The top part of the 'translation of tertiary requirements' form displays information on design attributes, their notation and defined target values. The bottom part of the form contains a matrix that displays the tertiary requirements and relative weights of tertiary requirements, as well as the notation for generated design attributes (DA01 to DA30).

The procedure for translating tertiary requirements into design attributes is similar to that for the calculation of tertiary requirements described earlier. It involves comparing tertiary requirements against each design attribute and determining whether there is any relationship between the two. The strength of the relationship between requirements and design attributes is specified by using either 9, 3, 1 or 0 to indicate strong relationship, some relationship, weak relationship and no relationship, respectively. The calculation of absolute (the sum-product of relative weights of tertiary requirements and the strength of the relationship between the two) and relative weights for design attributes, follows the same procedure for calculating the weights for tertiary

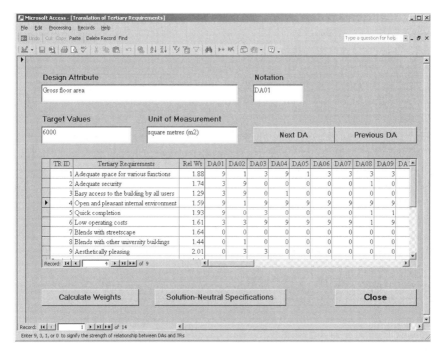

Figure 6.15. Mapping of tertiary requirements to design attributes

requirements. The relative weights for design attributes, together with design attributes and target values, make up the 'solution-neutral specifications', which are listed in the report shown in Figure 6.16. Solution-neutral specifications are the final output of the client requirements processing activity.

6.4.4   Comments on the use of ClientPro

The example run demonstrates the relative ease with which client requirements can be established using ClientPro. The tedious calculations of absolute and relative weights are performed automatically. The user is provided with adequate guidance on how to input and process information without the need to have mastered the methodology or computing environment on which ClientPro is based. Although the requirements for a building project were used in the example run, ClientPro can also be used for other project types, as there is enough

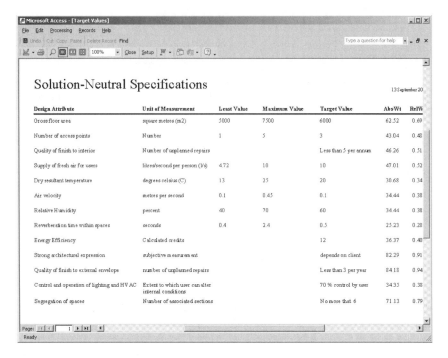

Figure 6.16. Report showing solution-neutral specifications

flexibility for the user to input information that is not necessarily geared towards a building.

6.5   Evaluation of ClientPro

To assess the effectiveness of ClientPro in facilitating the processing of client requirements, it was evaluated by a selection of industry practitioners who represent some of the potential users of the software. Four practitioners with an average of 14 years' experience in the construction industry were involved in the evaluation of ClientPro (Table 6.3).

Each evaluator was taken individually through the operation of ClientPro using the actual requirements for a building project, and was then requested to complete a questionnaire. The questionnaire was divided into three sections. Section A requested information about the evaluator's organisation, and about their position and experience. Section

Table 6.3. Details about evaluators and their organisations

Evaluator (respondent)		Organisation		
Position	Experience: years	Type of firm	Number of employees	Annual turnover: £ million
Chartered architect	20	Integrated practice (consultants)	160	6
Project manager	14	University (client)	4600	50
Planning and quality control manager	16	Mechanical and electrical (building services) contractors (contractors)	3200	350
Civil engineer	6	Consulting engineers (consultants)	1700	60
Total experience (years)	56	Total employees/ turnover	9660	466
Average experience (years)	14	Average employees/ turnover	2415	116·5

B contained a set of questions about various aspects of ClientPro, which were grouped into the following sub-headings:

- definition of requirements
- analysis of requirements
- translation of requirements into solution-neutral specifications
- management of requirements
- facilitation of team work
- relevance to the construction process
- a general section.

For each question, respondents were asked to express their opinion on the effectiveness of ClientPro on a scale of 1 (poor) to 5 (excellent). Section C requested comments on ways to improve the software, and for any other general comments. It should be mentioned that one of the evaluators was involved in the project whose requirements were used in the demonstration. Therefore, he had the opportunity to compare the briefing process for the actual project, and how the requirements could have been processed using ClientPro.

6.5.1   Evaluation results

All the evaluators were generally satisfied with the effectiveness of ClientPro in processing and managing client requirements, facilitating team work, being relevant to the needs of the industry and its general operation. Table 6.4 provides the average rankings of the effectiveness of ClientPro with respect to the specific questions in the evaluation questionnaire. It is evident that in most areas (e.g. precise definition of requirements, effective structuring of requirements, traceability of requirements, usefulness to the project team and the overall rating of the system) the effectiveness of ClientPro was given an average rating of at least 3·5 out of 5 (i.e. an effectiveness rating of 70% and over). The highest average rating of the system was 4 out of 5 (80%), and this was for the following areas:

- the extent to which design attributes are solution-neutral
- the translation of client requirements into design attributes
- the facilitation of a common understanding among members of the processing team
- the extent to which it represented an improvement on the existing process of briefing.

An average rating of 3·75 (i.e. 75%) was assigned to ClientPro for the following areas:

- the effectiveness of ClientPro in facilitating the precise definition of requirements
- the extent to which defined requirements are unambiguous
- realistic rankings for client requirements
- the facilitation of design creativity by the outputs of the system
- the ease of tracing requirements to the original intentions of the client
- the effective management of changes to requirements
- the usefulness of the system to the project team
- the overall rating of ClientPro.

An average rating of 3·5 (i.e. 70% effectiveness) was assigned for the following areas:

- the incorporation of the various perspectives represented by the client
- the effective structuring of requirements
- the accuracy of the rankings of interest groups represented by the client
- the usefulness of the solution-neutral specifications
- the relative ease to correlate and compare requirements
- the suitability of the system to existing procurement methods
- the effectiveness of the overall method for client requirements processing in ClientPro.

The lowest average ratings of 3 or 3·25 were found in the following areas:

- the facilitation of communication among members of the processing team
- the usefulness of the software to the overall construction process
- the ease of use of the system.

The low ratings in these three areas was probably due to less than appropriate wording (or varying interpretation) of the questions. For example, although 'facilitating communication' received a relatively low rating, the next question under that category (facilitating common understanding) received the highest average rating of 4. Similarly, the 'usefulness' of the system to the overall construction process received a rating of 3, but its usefulness to the project team received a rating of 3·75. This can be explained by the fact that although ClientPro was considered to be of 'benefit' to the construction process, its 'usefulness' was more pronounced at the requirements processing stage.

6.5.2   Suggestions for improvement and other comments

Table 6.5 presents the comments made by the evaluators on ways to improve ClientPro, and on what they felt about the system generally. The suggestions for improvement are focused mostly on the user interface. This reflects the relatively low average rating the system received with respect to ease of use. However, other comments by evaluators (for

Table 6.4. Responses to questions

Questions	Ranking (out of 5)	
	Average	Per cent
Definition of requirements		
1. How effectively does ClientPro facilitate the precise definition of requirements?	3·75	75
2. How well does it ensure that all the perspectives within the client are represented?	3·50	70
3. To what extent are the defined requirements unambiguous?	3·75	75
Analysis of requirements		
4. How effectively are requirements structured within ClientPro?	3·50	70
5. How accurate is the ranking of interest groups within the client?	3·50	70
6. How realistic are the rankings of client requirements?	3·75	75
Translation of requirements into solution-neutral specifications		
7. To what extent are design attributes solution-neutral?	4·00	80
8. How effectively are client requirements translated into design attributes?	4·00	80
9. How useful are the solution-neutral specifications?	3·50	70
10. To what extent would the outputs of ClientPro facilitate design creativity?	3·75	75

Management of requirements

11. How easy is it to trace requirements to the original intentions of the client?	3·75	75
12. How effectively are changes to requirements managed?	3·75	75
13. How easy is it to correlate and compare requirements in ClientPro?	3·50	70

Facilitation of teamwork

14. How well does ClientPro facilitate communication among members of the processing team?	3·25	65
15. How well does it facilitate a common understanding of the requirements among the team?	4·00	80

Relevance to the construction process

16. How useful is ClientPro to the overall construction process?	3·00	60
17. How useful is ClientPro to the project team?	3·75	75
18. To what extent does it represent an improvement to the existing briefing process?	4·00	80
19. How suitable is it to existing procurement methods?	3·50	70

General

20. How easy is ClientPro to use?	3·25	65
21. How effective is the overall method for client requirements processing in ClientPro?	3·50	70
22. What is your overall rating of the system	3·75	75

Table 6.5. General comments on ClientPro (some statements have been slightly edited to facilitate ease of reading)

Suggestions for improvement	Other comments
At some stages the presentation/graphics appeared cluttered and complex	For some clients/users of the software, the incorporation of services criteria (room temperatures, etc.) may be beyond their knowledge. While I can see clients using the software, I'm not sure they will be prepared to pay other consultants' fees to involve them in a project team. But in summary, ClientPro is an excellent tool to crystallise client requirements into a clearly defined and prioritised document
Maintain simplistic inputs and data; make sure system is easy to use at all times	
Perhaps clearer definition of user numbers (i.e. present and future)	
Weightings of user (interest) groups should not be available to all groups, to avoid political conflict	
A useful extension of the system would be a calculation of gross floor area required, although, as discussed, this would take considerable development	Thanks for letting me assess the software; I would like to try it on a new project perhaps later this year
	An excellent initiative
Ideally to be fully operational, make it a bit more user-friendly	Is there a manual?

example, 'an excellent tool' and 'an excellent initiative') indicate that, generally, they were very pleased with ClientPro.

6.6 ClientPro and the objectives for the CRPM

The development of ClientPro was aimed at facilitating the establishment of client requirements as specified in the CRPM. The goals for establishing client requirements, which were defined in Chapter 1, are as follows:

1. To address the complexities within the client body through the identification, resolution and incorporation of the different perspectives within the client body.
2. To clarify the objectives and expectations of the client to ensure that they are understood from the perspectives of the client.
3. To focus exclusively on client requirements so as to understand how other project requirements can either enhance or constrain their implementation.
4. To translate and present client requirements in a format that will allow collaborative working and the development, verification and management of appropriate design and construction solutions, which satisfy the objectives of the client.

The satisfaction of these goals requires that the client requirements are:

- clear and unambiguous to minimise/eliminate confusion and to facilitate verification and management of requirements
- represented in solution-neutral format and in a manner that facilitates understanding from different perspectives
- comprehensive (incorporating different perspectives and life-cycle issues)
- processed within an adequate framework to ensure that the required outputs are delivered
- processed within a computer-based environment.

The extent to which these objectives were satisfied by ClientPro is presented in Table 6.6, which links the questions in the questionnaire to the requirements for establishing client requirements. A calculation of the averages for the average ratings for each objective shows the following scores (out of 5):

- clear and unambiguous requirements — 3·67
- representation in solution-neutral format — 3·85
- comprehensive (incorporating different perspectives, etc.) — 3·58
- adequate framework to ensure required outputs are delivered — 3·50
- *average for all objectives* — 3·65.

These scores indicate that, although there is room for improvement, ClientPro does provide for the effective processing of client requirements

Table 6.6. ClientPro and the objectives for the CRPM

Objective	Questionnaire question	Average rating
Clear and unambiguous to minimise/eliminate confusion and to facilitate verification and management of requirements	How effectively does ClientPro facilitate the precise definition of requirements?	3·75
	To what extent are the defined requirements unambiguous?	3·75
	How effectively are requirements structured within ClientPro?	3·50
	How easy is it to trace requirements to the original intentions of the client?	3·75
	How effectively are changes to requirements managed?	3·75
	How easy is it to correlate and compare requirements in ClientPro?	3·50
	Average	*3·67*
Representation in solution-neutral format and in a manner that facilitates understanding from different perspectives	To what extent are design attributes solution-neutral?	4·00
	How effectively are client requirements translated into design attributes?	4·00
	How useful are the solution-neutral specifications?	3·50
	To what extent would the outputs facilitate design creativity?	3·75
	How well does it facilitate a common understanding of the requirements among the team?	4·00
	Average	*3·85*
Comprehensive (incorporating different perspectives and lifecycle issues)	How well does it ensure that all the perspectives within the client are represented?	3·50
	How accurate is the ranking of interest groups within the client?	3·50
	How realistic are the rankings of client requirements?	3·75
	Average	*3·58*

Table 6.6. continued

Objective	Questionnaire question	Average rating
Adequate framework to ensure required outputs are delivered	How well does ClientPro facilitate communication among members of the processing team?	3·25
	How useful is ClientPro to the project team?	3·75
	How useful is ClientPro to the overall construction process?	3·00
	To what extent does it represent an improvement to the existing process of briefing?	4·00
	How suitable is it to existing procurement methods?	3·50
	How easy is ClientPro to use?	3·25
	How effective is the overall method for client requirements processing in ClientPro?	3·50
	What is your overall rating of the system?	3·75
	Average	3·50

in construction. The evaluation also suggests that ClientPro, and the CRPM on which it is based, are of benefit to the client, the project team and, by implication, to the overall construction process.

Chapter 7

Summary and conclusions

7.1   Overview of Chapter 7

This chapter summarises the book and outlines the benefits of the client requirements processing model (CRPM) and ClientPro in the establishment of client requirements on construction projects. It concludes with a brief discussion on the methodology described in the book and suggests ways in which the CRPM and ClientPro can be extended.

7.2   General summary

The objective of this book was to present an innovative and structured approach for establishing the 'voice of the client' on construction projects. The need for an appropriate mechanism for establishing client requirements was identified, and the development of the methodology for client requirements processing was also described. What now follows is a summary of the main points covered in the preceding chapters.

7.2.1   Summary of Chapter 1

In Chapter 1, the context for establishing clients' requirements and some of the terminology used in the book were defined (e.g. client, 'voice of the client', etc.). The need and objectives for establishing the 'voice of the client' were established and the requirements for a suitable framework for client requirements processing were identified. The client was defined as an entity that incorporates other interest groups (e.g. users, etc.) and, therefore, it was considered appropriate to refer to the 'client body'. The importance of clients in the construction process (as initiators and financiers of construction projects, and as the driving force in the industry) was emphasised and the need for a clear definition of a client's requirements, as a first step towards client satisfaction and project success, was also stressed. The concept of the 'voice of the client' was defined to include the collective wishes, perspectives and expectations (i.e. requirements) of the various components of the client body. Following these definitions, other issues relating to the complexity of client organisations, the nature of their expectations, the nature of project requirements, and the need for integration and collaborative working to improve the efficiency of the construction industry, were explored. It was determined that, because of these issues, it was necessary that client requirements are effectively processed in order to:

- address the complexities within the client body through the identification, resolution and incorporation of the different perspectives within the client body
- clarify the objectives and expectations of the client to ensure that they are understood from the perspective of the client
- exclusively focus on client requirements so as to understand how other project requirements can either enhance or constrain their implementation
- translate and present client requirements in a format that will allow collaborative working and the development, verification and management of appropriate design and construction solutions, which satisfy the objectives of the client.

Therefore, it was necessary that the effective processing of client requirements should be done in a (preferably, computer-based) framework that facilitates:

- the processing of client requirements for different client and project types
- the identification, incorporation and prioritisation of the different perspectives within the client body through the use of appropriate elicitation and decision-making tools
- the participation and integration of multidisciplinary teams in defining the requirements of the client to eliminate, or minimise, the tendencies towards the 'over the wall' syndrome

- the capture, verification and management of all relevant information (e.g. issues relating to the lifecycle of the facility) pertaining to the objectives, needs and expectations of the client
- the integration of client requirements processing with other activities in the construction process.

Such a framework for requirements processing should ensure that client requirements are:

- clear and unambiguous, to minimise or eliminate any confusion arising from multiple interpretations of their meaning
- comprehensive (i.e. they should incorporate the collective wishes and of different components of the client, and issues relating to the lifecycle of the facility)
- solution-neutral, to allow innovation in devising solutions to the client's problem
- stated in a format that can be understood by the different disciplines working on a project.

The objectives and requirements for a framework that facilitates the establishment of client requirements on construction projects provided the basis for assessing the relevance of current briefing practices, and for developing a suitable methodology for client requirements processing.

7.2.2   Summary of Chapter 2

In Chapter 2, the current process of briefing in the UK construction industry was appraised to ascertain whether existing mechanisms for establishing client requirements satisfy the objectives for client requirements processing defined in Chapter 1. This appraisal was based on a detailed study of the briefing process that was carried out through literature reviews, case studies and a questionnaire survey of a sample of clients and consultants in the construction industry. This study revealed that:

- briefing is combined with conceptual and scheme design, and the brief evolves as the design gets progressively fixed
- a variety of methods (e.g. interviews, visits to similar facilities, etc.) are used to collect briefing information, which is sometimes documented in formal documents
- a process of 'trial and error', through the use of sketches and drawings, is used mostly to clarify the client's need

- although a broad mix of professionals can be involved in briefing, there is a tendency for design professionals (e.g. architects and engineers) to play a dominant role in briefing
- decision making in briefing is usually the result of discussions and negotiations between those involved in the briefing process
- briefing and design documents (e.g. sketches and drawings, minutes of meetings, etc.) are used to manage changes to requirements
- there is sufficient indication that the briefing process, as currently practised, is not considered to provide the optimum in defining and understanding the client's needs.

The study on briefing also established that the limitations in the briefing process, with respect to how well it contributes to the understanding and encapsulation of client requirements in the design and construction process, were due to:

- problems in the actual practice of briefing (e.g. inadequate involvement of all relevant parties, inadequate consideration of the perspectives represented by the client, inadequate communication between those involved in briefing, etc.)
- limitations in the framework for briefing (e.g. insufficient focus on client requirements, use of the solution to clarify the problem, inadequate provision for the traceability of requirements, etc.).

The findings on the process and limitations of the briefing process, together with related research on the subject, provided the basis for assessing the suitability of the current process of briefing in establishing client requirements according to the objectives set out in Chapter 1. This assessment concluded that the current process of briefing does not adequately support the effective processing of client requirements. In particular:

- using the design to clarify the client's objectives does not ensure that focus on client requirements is maintained, neither does it allow for the presentation of precisely defined requirements that incorporate lifecycle requirements for the proposed facility
- the use of sketches and drawings as the basis of reports at different stages in the briefing process does not represent an unambiguous 'statement' of the client's problem, which design is to solve, but a proposed solution to that problem

- the absence of a structured methodology for decision making can result in an inadequate incorporation of the perspectives and priorities of the client
- the use of design to properly define client requirements might tend to minimise the involvement of non-design professionals (e.g. quantity surveyors and facilities managers) in defining those requirements — this reinforces the sequential 'over the wall' approach and does not facilitate a concurrent approach to design.

It was further established that emerging attempts to improve the briefing process also do not satisfy the requirements for client requirements processing. Although some of these initiatives included computer-based solutions, they are focused mainly on automating current, flawed processes without any reengineering. Therefore, it was evident that the development of a methodology that addresses the requirements for establishing the 'voice of the client' on construction projects required further investigation into the processing of requirements in other disciplines, such as manufacturing, which has been used as a model of how the construction industry can be better improved.

7.2.3 Summary of Chapter 3

Chapter 3 explored different methodologies and tools that can be used to establish the 'voice of the client' on construction projects. The investigation into requirements processing in manufacturing and requirements engineering led to the identification of various tools and techniques that could facilitate the processing of client requirements. The identified techniques included:

- quality function deployment (QFD), a matrix-based methodology used in manufacturing to deploy the 'voice of the customer' in product development
- value tree analysis, similar to the function analysis system technique (FAST), which is used for the structuring of requirements
- decision-making techniques, such as criteria weighting (CW), and the weighted score model (WSM)
- computer-based tools, such as database applications and spreadsheet packages.

However, it was emphasised that these tools needed to be customised to suit the specific needs of the construction industry and should be integrated into a comprehensive methodology for establishing client requirements on construction projects.

7.2.4   Summary of Chapter 4

Chapter 4 described the methodology for establishing client requirements on construction projects, which is encapsulated in a client requirements processing model (CRPM). The development of the CRPM was based on a iterative process that involved discussions with practitioners in the construction industry. The process was based on a number of assumptions and capitalised on the opportunities within the construction industry, as well as the possibilities in adopting techniques from other disciplines for the effective processing of client requirements. The resulting model is a three-stage process as follows:

1. *Requirements definition* — this deals with the establishment and documentation of basic facts about the project and the client, identifying the groups/people that influence, or are affected by, the acquisition, operation and existence of the proposed facility, and eliciting the requirements of the client.
2. *Requirements analysis* — this involves the structuring of client requirements into primary, secondary and tertiary requirements, the prioritisation of interest groups and the prioritisation of tertiary requirements.
3. *Requirements translation* — this deals with the translation of client requirements into solution-neutral design specifications and involves the generation of design attributes, determination of target values for design attributes, association of tertiary requirements with design attributes and determining the strength of the relationship between them, and the prioritisation of design attributes.

The approach adopted in the model is the description of the facility that satisfies the business need of the client. This description is not based on the *physical* structure of the facility but with respect to its functions, attributes, effect on people and the environment, and the process of acquiring, operating and demolishing the facility. The focus is in generating solution-neutral specifications that will enhance the creativity of the design team, who are expected to design the physical structure that satisfies the requirements of the client. The activities incorporated in the three stages of the model are designed to satisfy the objectives for establishing client requirements defined in Chapter 1.

7.2.5   Summary of Chapter 5

Chapter 5 provided guidelines and examples of the practical application of the CRPM. The examples considered were a hypothetical family house project, an actual building project within a UK university and a bypass road project, all of which provided insights into the use of the model to establish client requirements on construction projects. Some considerations in the use of the CRPM to establish client requirements are as follows:

(a)   The role of the requirements processing team (RPT) is key to the application of the model because the CRPM is not intended to be a substitute for people and dialogue. Therefore, members of the RPT should be sufficiently knowledgeable of the construction process, and should comprise a mixture of disciplines that reflect the lifecycle of a facility. However, the size of the team will depend on the type and scale of the project under consideration.

(b)   The CRPM is intended to be used after the decision to build has been made, but before conceptual design. However, it was emphasised that the philosophy underpinning the model can be used in other stages of the construction process.

(c)   The CRPM can be used in a procurement route similar to that for design and build but it is also possible to use it in traditional contracting.

(d)   In eliciting client requirements, the focus should be on the articulated needs of clients, since basic needs, which deal mostly with baseline regulatory requirements, will have to be considered when designing and constructing the facility commissioned by the client. However, an adequate understanding of articulated needs can help in the discovery of 'exciting' needs that will pleasantly surprise the client.

(e)   Design attributes should have a broad relationship with tertiary requirements (i.e. they should be capable of those elements that can satisfy the wishes of clients). The use of the relationship matrix emphasises the fact that some design/technical specifications can address multiple client requirements

(*f*) Although the CRPM prescribes a systematic approach to the establishment of client requirements, this does not restrict iteration. On the contrary, it does enhance iteration by providing a structured means for tracing requirements as they are captured and processed.

(*g*) It was emphasised that the CRPM is designed to allow for the processing of client requirements without the use of sketches and other visual aids. However, it was acknowledged that their use might be unavoidable, for example, in the refurbishment of an existing facility, where drawings of the existing building will be used.

7.2.6 Summary of Chapter 6

Chapter 6 described the development, use and evaluation of ClientPro, which was designed to facilitate the establishment of client requirements according to the methodology prescribed in the CRPM. The process and information models of the CRPM in Chapter 4 provided the basis for the development of the prototype software, which was implemented as a MS Access application. The use of MS Access provided a relatively quick and effective way of demonstrating how client requirements can be processed in a computer environment, and the potential for its integration with other computer-based design and construction activities.

The chapter also reported on an evaluation of ClientPro by construction industry professionals following a demonstration of its use with the actual requirements of a building project (the university building project example in Chapter 5). The evaluation confirmed that, in spite of the improvements required to make ClientPro fully operational, it does proffer many benefits in facilitating the establishment of client requirements on construction projects.

7.3 Benefits of the client requirements processing model and ClientPro

7.3.1 Direct benefits

The direct benefits of the CRPM (and ClientPro) derive from its use in facilitating the effective processing of client requirements. In particular:

- it helps clients to clarify their vision of the facility to be constructed
- it ensures that client requirements are defined clearly at an early stage
- it facilitates communication and a common understanding of the client's requirements among members of the RPT and, subsequently, those of the design team
- it enhances collaborative working because of the common understanding of the client's requirements among members of the design team
- it facilitates design creativity since client requirements are translated into a solution-neutral format
- it minimises uncertainties due to the precise definition of client requirements
- it can contribute to the minimisation of downstream problems due to early consideration of issues affecting the lifecycle of the proposed facility
- it provides the basis for effective requirements management throughout the project lifecycle
- it provides a first step to complete client satisfaction because of precise and unambiguous definition of client requirements
- it represents an improved alternative to the existing process of briefing — a comparison between current briefing practice and the methodology in the CRPM is provided in Table 7.1.

7.3.2 Indirect benefits

In facilitating collaborative working in construction, the CRPM is of benefit to the industry because of the associated benefits in adopting a collaborative mode of working. These benefits include:

- the enhancement of teamwork with better coordination of the efforts of team members
- the consideration of lifecycle issues at the requirements stage can facilitate the incorporation of buildability, safety and risk analyses during the design process
- the precise definition of client requirements can facilitate the clear allocation of risks and, therefore, can minimise disputes and claims inherent in the conventional procedure for design and construction
- the design and construction of facilities that precisely match client needs.

Table 7.1. Comparison between the CRPM and current briefing practice

Establishing client requirements with the CRPM	Current briefing practice
Client requirements processing is done before conceptual design	Briefing is combined with design
Problem-focused approach whereby requirements are sufficiently defined before conceptual design starts	Solution-focused approach is usually adopted. The 'solution', in the form of sketches/drawings, is used to define the problem
Client requirements processing is done by a team (the RPT), which comprises representatives of the client and appointed construction professionals	Briefing is usually the responsibility of the architect and the client representative(s). No deliberate effort to include other 'downstream' professionals (e.g. engineers, contractors, suppliers, etc.) at the briefing stage
Structured approach to the prioritisation of client requirements using formal decision-making techniques	Prioritisation is done through discussions. There is no formal approach to prioritisation

7.4 Concluding comments

The CRPM (and ClientPro) represents a unique and innovative approach to the establishment of client requirements. It serves as an intermediate stage for the systematic analysis and mapping of client needs to design specifications. Thus, it provides an effective means of bridging the gap (e.g. terminology, focus and perspective) between clients and the construction industry. The CRPM also ensures that adequate focus on client requirements is maintained. This was achieved by the adoption of an approach that focuses on describing the proposed facility (which satisfies the business need of the client) in terms of its functions, attributes, effect on people and the environment, and the process of acquiring, operating and possible demolition of the facility.

The guidelines and examples on the use of the CRPM are intended to facilitate the effective use of the model. However, there are challenges and limitations of which users should be aware. For example, the identification and prioritisation of interest groups can be quite challenging because a group will not want to be considered as less important than other groups. Eliciting the preferences of external groups can also be problematic. But it was noted that projects that tend to attract strong concerns from external groups (e.g. road projects and controversial greenfield developments) do have public enquiries that provide an adequate forum for assessing the preferences of such groups. Another consideration for users is that using the CRPM is not necessarily a 'one-day' affair, as some aspects of weightings, etc., might need to be investigated over a number of days/weeks.

The implementation of the model requires that sufficient time is allowed for requirements processing. Since this is at odds with the current culture in the construction industry (where insufficient time is spent in defining client requirements), this approach might not be welcome by some sectors of the industry. Furthermore, if the model is implemented by a design team, they may be constrained by design deadlines, and may consider the approach represented by the model to be unnecessary. Indeed, the model was designed to be implemented by a separate RPT. This might be an additional cost to the client but this cost is expected to be no more that is usually expended in commissioning an architect to develop an initial design. Also, since downstream changes can be minimised, it is good value for money and, potentially, will result in overall cost reduction and increased client satisfaction.

It should be noted that client requirements, in themselves, are not sufficient for design. They need to be combined with other project requirements, such as site information and regulatory requirements, in order to provide a comprehensive set of design requirements (i.e. to present both the problem and context for design). It should also be emphasised that the establishment of client requirements is no guarantee that the resulting facility will fully satisfy the client. Other factors, such as the skill of designers and constructors, and the quality of materials used in construction do contribute to the creation of a facility that excites a client. The effective management of client requirements (e.g. monitoring compliance to requirements, etc.) during the course of the project and throughout the lifecycle of a facility also contributes to achieving the client's objectives for a facility. However, establishing and incorporating the 'voice of the client' in the design and construction process is a vital first step towards the design and construction of facilities that precisely match, and possibly exceed, the client's needs and expectations.

Further work in the following areas can serve to enhance the methodology described in this book:

(*a*) Further improvements and extensions to ClientPro, for example, into a distributed web-based application, and the incorporation of comprehensive online help facilities. Extending ClientPro to include the capture of other project requirements will also enhance its usability.

(*b*) The integration of ClientPro with conceptual design, so that solution-neutral design specifications are mapped directly on to design concepts.

(*c*) Developing and integrating ClientPro into a comprehensive system for managing client requirements throughout the lifecycle of a facility.

Finally, it must be emphasised that the CRPM (and ClientPro) is a vital tool that can assist the construction industry to understand clearly the needs of its clients. This is a key ingredient of a client-focused industry that delivers facilities that meet clients' requirements. Its use by industry practitioners is therefore encouraged.

References

Ahmed, S. M. and Kangari, R. (1995). Analysis of Client-Satisfaction Factors in the construction industry. *Journal of management in Engineering,* **11,** No. 2, March/April, 36–44.

Akao, Y. (1990a). History of Quality Function Deployment in Japan. In Zeller, H. J. (ed.), *The Best on Quality: Targets, Improvements, Systems.* Hanser Publishers, New York, pp. 184–196.

Akao, Y. (1990b). An Introduction to Quality Function Deployment. In Akao, Y. (ed.), *Quality Function Deployment (QFD): Integrating Customer Requirements into Product Design.* Productivity Press, Massachusetts, pp. 1–24.

Akao, Y. (1997). QFD: Past, Present, and Future. In Gustafsson, A., Bergman, B. and Ekdahl, F. (eds), *Proceedings of the Third Annual International QFD Symposium,* Vol. 1, Linkoping, Sweden, 1–2 October, pp. 19–29.

Akomode, O. J., Lees, B. and Irgens, C. (1998). Constructing Customised Models and Providing Information to Support IT Outsourcing Decisions. *Logistics Information and Management,* **11,** No. 2, 114–127.

Anumba, C. J. and Evbuomwan, N. F. O. (1997). Concurrent Engineering in Design-Build Projects. *Construction Management and Economics,* **15,** No. 3, 271–281.

Anumba, C. J., Evbuomwan, N. F. O. and Sarkodie-Gyan, T. (1995). An approach to Modelling Construction as a Competitive Manufacturing Process. *Proceedings of the 12th Conference of the Irish Manufacturing Committee,* Cork, pp. 1069–1076.

Architects' Journal (1980). Failures in Brief (Leader). *Architects' Journal,* 19 November.

Ashworth, A. (1991). *Contractual Procedures in the Construction Industry,* 2nd edition. Longman, London.

Barrett, P. (1996). *Managing the Brief.* Paper presented at the Royal Institute of British Architects/Innovative Manufacturing Initiative (RIBA/IMI) Seminar on Briefing, 16 October, 1999, London.

Brandon, P. and Betts, M. (1995). The field of integrated construction information: and editorial overview. In Brandon, P. and Betts, M. (eds), *Integrated Construction Information.* E & FN Spon, London.

British Property Federation (BPF) (1983). *The British Property Federation (BPF) System for the Design of Buildings.* BPF, UK.

Britton, C. and Doake, J. (1996). *Software System Development: A Gentle Introduction.* McGraw-Hill, London.

Bryman, A. (1989). *Research Methods and Organisation Studies.* Unwin Hyman, London.

Bypass (2000). *The Newbury Bypass Factfile.* http://www.geocities.com/newbury bypass/index.html (accessed 1 February 2002).

Cherns, A. B. and Bryant, D. T. (1984). Studying the client's role in construction management. *Construction Management and Economics,* Vol. 2, pp. 177–184.

Chung, E. K. (1989). A Survey of Process Modeling Tools. *Technical Report No. 7,* CIC Research Program, Pennsylvania State University, Pennsylvania.

Clausing, D. (1997). Product Development. In Gustafsson, A., Bergman, B. and Ekdahl, F. (eds), *Proceedings of the Third Annual International QFD Symposium,* Vol. 1, Linkoping, Sweden, 1–2 October, pp. 31–55.

Construction Industry Board (CIB) (1997). *Briefing the Team.* CIB, Thomas Telford Publishing , London.

Construction Industry Council (CIC) (1997). *Building for Energy Efficiency: The Client's Briefing Guide.* CIC, London.

Construct IT (CIT) (1996). *Benchmarking Best Practice Report: Briefing and Design.* CIT Centre of Excellence, Salford (ISBN 1-900491-33-8).

Contracts Journal (1995). Monthly editions of the *Contracts Journal,* UK.

Crowley, A. (1996). Construction as a Manufacturing Process. In Kumar, B. and Retik, A. (eds), *Information Representation and Delivery in Civil and Structural Engineering Design,* CIVIL-COMP PRESS, Edinburgh, Scotland, pp. 85–91.

Davis, P. A. (1995). QFD — A Structured Approach to Understanding the Voice of the Customer. *IEEE Applied Power Electronic Conference and Exposition,* Piscataway, New Jersey, Vol. 1, pp. 245–251 (ISS 95CH35748).

Day, R. G. (1993). Using Quality Function Deployment in the Product Development Process. *Journal of Applied Manufacturing Systems,* Fall, 28–39.

Dean, E. B. (1992). Quality Function Deployment for Large Systems. *International Engineering Management Conference: Management in the Global Environment*, Sheraton Hotel and Conference Centre, Eatontown, New Jersey, 25–28 October, pp. 317–321.

Department of the Environment (1995a). *Construct IT — Bridging the Gap*. HMSO, London.

Department of the Environment (1995b). *Construction Quality: A strategy for quality in construction*. DOE Consultative Document, London.

Dynamic Object Oriented Requirements System (DOORS) (1997). http://www.telelogic.com/products/doors/ (accessed 1 February 2002).

Egan, J. (1998). Rethinking Construction. *Report of the Construction Task Force on the Scope for Improving the Quality and Efficiency of UK Construction*, Department of the Environment, Transport and the Regions, London.

Evbuomwan, N. F. O. (1994). *Design Function Deployment: A Concurrent Engineering Design System*. PhD thesis, City University, London.

Evbuomwan, N. F. O. and Anumba, J. C. (1995). Concurrent Life-Cycle Design and Construction. In Topping, B. H. V. (ed.), *Developments in Computer Aided Design and Modelling for Civil Engineering*. CIVIL-COMP PRESS, Edinburgh, UK, pp. 93–102.

Evbuomwan, N. F. O. and Anumba, J. C. (1996a). Towards an Integrated Engineering Design Environment. In Kumar , B. and Retik, A. (eds), *Information Representation and Delivery in Civil and Structural Engineering*. CIVIL-COMP PRESS, Edinburgh, pp. 127–134.

Evbuomwan, N. F. O. and Anumba, J. C. (1996b). Towards a Concurrent Engineering Model for Design-and-Build Projects. *The Structural Engineer*, **74**, No. 5, 73–78.

Fiksel, J. and Hayes-Roth, F. (1993). Computer-Aided Requirements Management. *Concurrent Engineering: Research and Applications*, **1**, 83–92.

Fowlkes, W. Y. and Creveling, C. M. (1995). *Engineering Methods for Robust Design: Using Taguchi Methods in Technology and Product Development*. Addison-Wesley Publishing Company, Massachusetts.

Freeman, P. (1980). Requirements Analysis and Specification: The First Step. *Advances in Computer Technology*, pp. 290–296.

Gause, D. C. and Weinberg, G. M. (1989). *Exploring Requirements: Quality Before Design*. Dorset House Publishing, New York.

Gibson Jr., G. E., Kaczmarowski, J. H. and Lore Jr., H. E. (1995). Pre-project Planning Process for Capital Facilities. *Journal of Construction Engineering and Management*, **121**, No. 3, 312–318.

Goodacre, P., Pain, J., Murray, J. and Noble, M. (1982). *Research in Building Design*. Occasional Paper No. 7, Department of Construction Management, University of Reading.

Griffin, A. and Hauser, J. R. (1991). The Voice of the Customer. *Working Paper*, Sloan School of Management, Massachusetts Institute of Technology.

Griffith, A. and Headley, J. D. (1997). Using the Weighted Score Model as an Aid to Selecting Procurement Methods for Small Building Works. *Construction Management and Economics*, **15**, 341–348.

Gustafsson, A., Bergman, B. and Ekdahl, F. (eds) (1997). *Proceedings of the Third Annual International QFD Symposium*, Vols. 1 and 2, Linkoping, Sweden, 1–2 October.

Hague, P. (1993). *Questionnaire Design*. Kogan Page Limited, London.

Halbleib, L., Wormington, P., Cieslak, W. and Street, H. (1993). Application of Quality Function Deployment to the Design of a Lithium Battery, pp. 150–154.

Hasdogan, G. (1996). The Role of User Models in Product Design for Assessment of User Needs. *Design Studies*, **17**, 19–33.

Hauser, J. R. (1993). How Puritan-Bennett Used the House of Quality. *Sloan Management Review*, Spring, 61–70.

Hauser, J. R. and Clausing, D. (1988). The House of Quality. *Harvard Business Review*, May–June, 63–73.

Hellard, R. B. (1993). *Total Quality in Construction Projects*, Thomas Telford Publishing, London.

Highways Agency (2000). *Route Management Strategy Guidance* (available at http://www.highways.gov.uk/info/rootstrat/index.htm — accessed 1 February 2002).

Howard, H. C., Lewitt, R. E., Paulson, B. C., Pohl, J. G. and Tatum, C. B. (1989). Computer Integration: Reducing Fragmentation in AEC Industry. *Journal of Computing in Civil Engineering*, **3**, No. 1, Jan., 18–32.

Howie, W. (1996). Controlling the Client. *New Civil Engineer*, 17 October, pp. 12.

Huovila, P., Lakka, A., Laurikka, P. and Vainio, M. (1997). Involvement of Customer Requirements in Building Design. In Alarcon, L. (ed.), *Lean Construction*. A. A. Balkema, Rotterdam, pp. 403–416.

Integrated Definition (IDEF) (1993). Integration Definition for Function Modelling (IDEF0). *Federal Information Processing Standards (FIPS) Publication 183*. National Institute of Standards and Technology, USA.

Institution of Civil Engineers (ICE) (1996a). *Civil Engineering Procedure*, 4th edition. Thomas Telford Publishing, London.

Institution of Civil Engineers (ICE) (1996b). *Creating Value in Engineering — Institution of Civil Engineers (ICE) Design and Practice Guides*, Thomas Telford Publishing, London.

Institution of Civil Engineers (ICE) (1997). Newbury Bypass. *Briefing Sheets* (available at http://www.icenet.org.uk/icenews/brstory.asp?title=8&Button=BriefingSheets — accessed September 2001).

International Standards Organisation (ISO) (1992). *Building Construction — Expression of Users' Requirements (ISO 6242 Parts 1–3)*. ISO, Geneva, Switzerland.

International Standards Organisation (ISO) (1994). *ISO 10303-11: Industrial Automation Systems and Integration — Product Data Representation and Exchange — Part 11: Description Methods: The EXPRESS Language Reference Manual*. ISO, Geneva, Switzerland.

Johnston, G. O. and Burrows, D. J. (1995). Keeping the Customer Really Satisfied. *GEC Review*, **10**, No. 1, 31–39.

Kamara, J. M. and Anumba, C. J. (2001). A Critical Appraisal of the Briefing Process in Construction. *Journal of Construction Research*, **2**, No. 1, 13–24.

Kamara, J, M., Anumba, C. J. and Evbuomwan, N. F. O. (1996). *A Review of Existing Mechanisms for Processing Clients Requirements in the Construction Industry*. Technical Report No. 96/1, School of Science and Technology, University of Teesside (ISBN 0 907550 75 4).

Kamara, J. M., Anumba, C. J. and Evbuomwan, N. F. O. (1998). Tools for Client Requirements Processing in Concurrent Life-Cycle Design and Construction. In Horvath, I. and Taleb-Bendiab, A. (eds), *Proceedings of the 2nd International Symposium on Tools and Methods for Concurrent Engineering*, Manchester, 21–23 April, pp. 73–83.

Kamara, J. M., Anumba, C. J. and Evbuomwan, N. F. O. (1999). Client Requirements Processing in Construction: A New Approach Using QFD. *ASCE Journal of Architectural Engineering*, **5**, No. 1, 8–15.

Kamara, J. M., Anumba, C. J. and Evbuomwan, N. F. O. (2000). Establishing and processing client requirements — a key aspect of concurrent engineering in construction. *Engineering, Construction and Architectural Management*, **7**, No. 1, 15–28.

Kelly, J., MacPherson, S. and Male, S. (1992). *The Briefing Process: A Review and Critique*. Paper No. 12, Royal Institution of Chartered Surveyors, UK (ISBN 0-85406-541-5).

Khorramshahgol, R. and Moustakis, V. S. (1988). Delphic Hierarchy Process (DHP): A Methodology for Priority Setting Derived from the Delphi Method and Analytical Hierarchy Process. *European Journal of Operational Research*, **37**, 347–354.

Kometa, S. T. and Olomolaiye, P. O. (1997). Evaluation of Factors Influencing Construction Clients' Decision to Build. *Journal of Management in Engineering*, **13**, No. 2, 77–86.

Kometa, S. T., Olomolaiye, P. O. and Harris, F. C. (1995). An evaluation of clients' needs and responsibilities in the construction process. *Engineering, Construction and Architectural Management*, **2**, No. 1, 57–76.

Kott, A. and Peasant, J. L. (1995). Representation and Management of Requirements: The RAPID-WS Project. *Concurrent Engineering: Research and Applications*, **3**, No. 2, 93–106.

Kumar, B. (1996). *A Prototype Design Brief Development Assistant*. MSc dissertation, University of Glasgow.

Latham, M. (1994). Construction the Team. *Final Report on Joint Review of Procurement and Contractual Arrangements in the UK Construction Industry*, HMSO, London.

Lawson, B. (1997). *How Designers Think: The Design Process Demystified*. Architectural Press, Oxford.

Lin, Z-C. and Shieh, T-J. (1995). Application of an Analytical Hierarchy Process Method and Fuzzy Compositional Evaluation in the Expert System of Sheet Bending Design. *International Journal of Advanced Manufacturing Technology*, **10**, No. 1, 3–10.

Lin, J., Fox, M. S. and Bilgic, T. (1996). A Requirements Ontology for Engineering for Engineering Design. In Sobolewski, M. and Fox, M. (eds), *Advances in Concurrent Engineering: Proceedings of the CE96 Conference*, pp. 343–351.

Lochner, R. H. and Matar, J. E. (1990). *Designing for Quality: An Introduction to the Best of Taguchi and Western Methods of Statistical Experimental Design*. Chapman and Hall, New York.

Lockamy III, A. and Khurana, A. (1995). Quality Function Deployment: A Case Study. *Production and Inventory Management Journal*, second quarter, 56–60.

MacLeod, I. A., Kumar, K. and McCullough, J. (1998). Innovative Design in the Construction Industry. *Proceedings of the Institution of Civil Engineers, Civil Engineering*, **126**, 31–38.

Maddux, G. A., Amos, R. W. and Wyskida, A. R. (1991). Organisations can apply Quality Function Deployment as a Strategic Planning Tool. *Industrial Engineering*, September, 33–37.

Mallon, J. C. and Mulligan, D. E. (1993). Quality Function Deployment — A System for Meeting Customers' Needs. *Journal of Construction Engineering and Management*, **119**, No. 3, 516–531.

McLaren, B. J. (1996). *Understanding and Using Microsoft Access for Windows 95*. West Publishing Company, Minneapolis, USA.

Miles, L. D. (1972). *Techniques of Value Analysis and Engineering*. McGraw-Hill, New York.

Miller, D. C. (1991). *Handbook of Research Design and Social Measurement*, 5th edition. Sage Publications, USA.

Miyatake, Y. and Kangari, R. (1993). Experiencing Computer Integrated Construction. *Journal of Construction Engineering and Management*, **119**, No. 2, 307–322.

Morris, J., Rogerson, J. and Jared, G. (1998). A Tool for Modelling the Briefing and Design Decision Making Processes in Construction. In Hughes, W. (ed.), *Proceedings of the 14th Annual Conference of the Association of Researchers in Construction Management*, Association of Researchers in Construction Management, UK, 320–329.

Mitsufugi, Y. and Uchida, T. *et al.* (1990). Using and Promoting Quality Charts. In Akao, Y. (ed.), *Quality Function Deployment (QFD): Integrating Customer Requirements into Product Design*. Productivity Press, Massachusetts.

New Civil Engineer (NCE) (1996). *Consultants File 1996*. Supplement to the *New Civil Engineer* magazine.

Newman, R., Jenks, M., Dawson, S. and Bacon, V. (1981). *Brief Formulation and the Design of Buildings: A Report of a Pilot Study*. Buildings Research Team, Department of Architecture, Oxford Brookes University.

Palmer, M. A. (1981). *The Architect's Guide to Facility Programming*. America Institute of Architects, New York.

Paredes, C. and Fiadeiro, J. L. (1995). Reuse of Requirements and Specifications: A Formal Framework. *Association of Computing Machniery (ACM) Sigsoft Symposium on Software Reliability*, New York, ISS Conference No. 43715, pp. 263–266.

Parsloe, C. J. (1990). A Design Briefing Manual. *Application Guide 1/90*, Building Services Research Institute Association (BSRIA), UK (ISBN 0 86022 266 7).

Perkinson, G. M., Sanvido, V. E. and Grobler, F. (1994). A Facility Programming Information Framework. *Engineering, Construction and Architectural Management*, **1**, No. 1, pp. 69–84.

Prasad, B. (1996). Concurrent Function Deployment — An Emerging Alternative to QFD: Conceptual Framework. In Sobolewski, M. and Fox, M. (eds), *Advances in Concurrent Engineering: Proceedings of CE96 Conference.* Technomic Publishing Company, USA, pp.105–112.

Ramesh, B., Dwiggins, D., DeVries, G. and Edwards, M. (1995). Towards Requirements Traceability Models. *International Symposium and Workshop of Systems Engineering of Computer Based Systems,* ISS Conference, No. 43126, pp. 229–232.

Ranky, P. G. (1994). *Concurrent/Simultaneous Engineering (Methods, Tools and Case Studies).* CIMware Limited, UK.

Rational Rose (1998). Rational RequisitePro, A Rational Suite Product (available at http://www.rational.com/products/reqpro/ — accessed 1 February 2002).

Ross, D. T. and Schoman Jr., K. E. (1977). Structured Analysis for Requirements Definition. *IEEE Transactions on Software Engineering,* Vol. SE-3, No. 1, pp. 6–15.

Royal Institute of British Architects (RIBA) (1973). *Plan of Work for Design Team Operation.* Reprinted from the *RIBA Handbook,* RIBA, London.

Royal Institute of British Architects (RIBA) (1995). *RIBA Directory of Practices in the UK, 1995.* RIBA, London.

Rudduck, L. (1995). *Quantitative Methods for the Built Environment, Vol. 1: Statistical Analysis.* White Castle Press, Warrington.

Saaty, T. L. (1982). The Analytic Hierarchy Process: A New Approach to deal with Fuzziness in Architecture. *Architectural Science Review,* **25**, No. 3, 64–69.

Saaty, T. L. (1990). *The Analytic Hierarchy Process,* 2nd edition. RWS Publications, USA.

Saaty, T. L. and Beltran, M. H. (1980). Architectural Design by the Analytic Hierarchy Process. *Design Methods and Theories,* **14**, No. 3/4, 124–134.

Salisbury, F. (1990), *Architect's Handbook for Client Briefing.* Butterworth Architecture, London.

Sanvido, V. E. and Medeiros, D. J. (1990). Applying Computer-Integrated Manufacturing Concepts to Construction. *Journal of Construction Engineering and Management,* **116**, No. 2, 365–379.

Sanvido, V. E. and Norton, K. J. (1994). Integrated Design-Process Model. *Journal of Management in Engineering,* **10**, No. 5, 55–62.

Sanvido, V. E., Khayyal, S., Guvenis, M., *et al.* (1990). An Integrated Building Process Model. *Technology Report No. 1,* CIC Research Program, Pennsylvania State University, University Part, Pennsylvania.

Sanvido, V. E., Grobler, F., Parfitt, K., Guvenis, M. and Coyle, M. (1992). Critical Success Factors for Construction Projects. *Journal of Construction Engineering and Management,* **118**, No. 1, 94–111.

Serpell, A. and Wagner, R. (1997). Application of Quality Function Deployment (QFD) to the Determination of the Design Characteristics of Building Apartments. In Alarcón, L. (ed.), *Lean Construction*. A. A. Balkema, Rotterdam, pp. 355–363.

Serpell, A. and Wagner, R. (1997). Application of Quality Function Deployment (QFD) to the Determination of the Design Characteristics of Building Apartments. In Alarcón, L. (ed.), *Lean Construction*. A. A. Balkema, Rotterdam, pp. 355–363.

Sharpe, D. E. (1972). *The Design Process in Civil Engineering*. MSc thesis, Loughborough University.

Shiino, J. and Nishihara, R. (1990). Quality Development in the Construction Industry. In Akao, Y. (ed.), *Quality Function Deployment (QFD): Integrating Customer Requirements into Product Design*. Productivity Press, Massachusetts, pp. 263–297.

Sivaloganathan, S. and Evbuomwan, N. F. O. (1997). Quality Function Deployment — The Technique: State of the Art and Future Directions. *Concurrent Engineering: Research and Applications*, **5**, No. 2, 171–181.

Som, R. K. (1973). *A Manual of Sampling Techniques*. Heineman, London.

Stevens, R. and Martin, J. (1997). *What is Requirements Management?* http://www.telelogic.com/industries/milaero/papers.cfm (accessed 1 February 2002).

Stevens, R. and Putlock, G. (1997). *Improving Requirements Management*. http://www.telelogic.com/industries/milaero/papers.cfm (accessed 1 February 2002).

Taschek, J. (1997). *Relational Databases are Not Enough Anymore*. http://www.telelogic.com/download/paper/relational.pdf (accessed 1 February 2002).

Tran, T-L. and Sherif, J. S. (1995). Quality Function Deployment (QFD): An Effective Technique for Requirements Acquisition and Reuse. *Proceedings of the IEEE International Software Engineering Standards Symposium*, Los Alomitos, California, pp. 191–200.

Tseng. M. M. and Jiao, J. (1998). Computer-Aided Requirements Management for Product Definition: A Methodology and Implementation. *Concurrent Engineering: Research and Applications*, **6**, No. 2, 145–160.

Tummala, V. M. R., Chin, K. S. and Ho, S. H. (1996). Assessing Success Factors for Implementing CE: A Case Study in the Hong Kong Plastic Products Industry Using AHP. In Sobolewski, M. and Fox, M. (eds), *Advances in Concurrent Engineering: Proceedings of CE96 Conference*, Technomic Publishing Company, USA, pp. 395–402.

Ulrich, K. T. and Eppinger, S. D. (1995). *Product Design and Development*. McGraw-Hill, New York.

Vilela, R. M. and Cheng, L. C. (1997). QFD and CE: A Successful Arrangement. In Gustafsson, A., Bergman, B. and Ekdahl, F. (eds), *Proceedings of the Third Annual International QFD Symposium*, Vol. 1, Linkoping, Sweden, 1–2 October, pp. 199–212.

Walker, A. (1989). *Project Management in Construction*, 2nd edition. BSF Professional Books, UK.

Winter, J. (1989). New Roles in Contracting. In Uff, J. and Capper, P. (eds), *Construction Contract Policy: Improved Procedures and Practice*. Centre of Construction Law and Management, King's College, London.

Worthington, J. (1994). Effective Project Management Results from Establishing the Optimum Brief. *Property Review*, November, 182–185.

Yusuf, F. (1997). *Information and Process Modeling for Effective IT Implementation at the Briefing Stage*. PhD thesis, University of Salford.

Zahedi, F. (1986). The Analytic Hierarchy Process. *Interfaces*, **16** No. 4, 96–108.

Zave, P. (1995). Classification of Research Efforts in Requirements Engineering. *Proceedings of the IEEE International Conference on Requirements Engineering*, ISS 95th 8040, pp. 214–216.

Index